Global Wage Report 2014/15

Wages and income inequality

International Labour Organization

The International Labour Organization (ILO) was founded in 1919 to promote social justice and thereby contribute to universal and lasting peace. The ILO is responsible for drawing up and overseeing international labour standards. It is the only tripartite United Nations agency that brings together representatives of governments, employers and workers to jointly shape policies and programmes promoting decent work for all. This unique arrangement gives the ILO an edge in incorporating "real world" knowledge about employment and work.

Global Wage Report 2014/15

Wages and income inequality

INTERNATIONAL LABOUR OFFICE • GENEVA
ACADEMIC FOUNDATION • NEW DELHI

First published in 2015 by

International Labour Office,
CH-1211 Geneva 22, Switzerland
www.ilo.org

in association with

Academic Foundation
(co-publication partners for South Asia)
4772/23 Bharat Ram Road, (23 Ansari Road), Darya Ganj,
New Delhi - 110002, India.
www.academicfoundation.org

Global Wage Report 2014/15: Wages and income inequality

International Labour Office – Geneva: ILO, 2015

ISBN 978-92-2-128664-6 (print)
ISBN 978-92-2-128665-3 (web pdf)
ISBN 978-92-2-128666-0 (epub)

International Labour Office

wages / income distribution / wage differential / wage policy / developed countries / developing countries

13.07

Also available in PDF in Arabic: ISBN 978-92-2-628665-8; Chinese: ISBN 978-92-2-528665-9; French: ISBN 978-92-2-228665-2; Portuguese: ISBN 978-92-2-828665-6; Russian: ISBN 978-92-2-428665-0; and Spanish: ISBN 978-92-2-328665-1.

Also available as EPUB in French: ISBN 978-92-2-228666-9; and Spanish: ISBN 978-92-2-328666-8.
Also available in Kindle and iBook edition.

ILO Cataloguing in Publication Data

ISBN 978-93-327-0189-2 (Academic Foundation / for South Asia)

Printed and bound in India.

Preface

The *Global Wage Report 2014/15* presents both the latest trends in average wages and an analysis of the role of wages in income inequality. The first part of the report shows that global wage growth in recent years was driven by emerging and developing economies, where real wages have been rising since 2007 although wage growth slowed in 2013 compared to 2012. In developed economies, wages generally remained stagnant in 2012 and 2013, and in a number of countries wages remained below their 2007 level. These trends are a matter of concern.

At the level of the individual worker or firm, the immediate impacts of higher or lower wages are self-evident. At the national level, the effects of higher or lower wages on aggregate demand and employment are context-specific and cannot be predicted or evaluated without taking into account the level of wages relative to productivity, the degree of openness of the country under consideration and the relative size of the different components of aggregate demand. At the international level, if too many countries pursue wage moderation policies, the outcome is likely to be negative. In the current environment, in which the global economy risks sliding back into a low-growth trap, higher wage growth would be desirable in those countries where wages in the past have lagged behind productivity growth. As the report demonstrates, in some countries policies have already started to shift in that direction.

The second part of the report turns to the role of wages in income inequality. Inequality has become the subject of growing interest in recent years across the world, and there has been a realization that growing inequality not only undermines social justice objectives, but can also have adverse economic consequences. Through the adoption of the 2008 Declaration on Social Justice for a Fair Globalization, ILO Members renewed their commitment to pursue policies with regard to wages and earnings designed to ensure a just share of the fruits of progress to all and recognized that for a fair outcome for all, it has become even more necessary to achieve social cohesion and to combat poverty and rising inequalities.

In many countries, the distribution of wages and paid employment has been a key factor in recent inequality trends. This highlights the importance of labour market institutions and policies – including minimum wages and collective bargaining – that have an effect on income distribution.

Wage gaps between men and women, and between nationals and migrants, remain significant and are only partly explained by differences in experience, education, occupation and other labour market characteristics. Implementing effective anti-discrimination policies, alongside other policies that address the underlying causes of these wage gaps, is a concrete way to progress toward greater social justice and fewer inequalities.

The report also shows that lower-income groups rely disproportionately on social transfers or income from self-employment. In fact, in almost all countries, income sources are more diverse at the top and bottom of the household income distribution than in the middle, where households rely to a much larger extent on wages. This illustrates the importance of ensuring coherence between wage policies and social protection alongside the creation of paid employment to reduce inequality.

It is my hope that, in addition to the report itself, the approach presented here will be of use for ILO constituents to identify, in their specific context, the appropriate mix of wages, employment, enterprise promotion, social protection and other policies that are most conducive to combining increased economic growth with decreased income inequality. It is also my hope that the report will assure policy-makers of the importance of including wages as part of international efforts to coordinate macroeconomic policies and to advance social justice.

Guy Ryder
ILO Director-General

Contents

Figures

Boxes

Appendix figures

Appendix tables

Appendix boxes

Acknowledgements

Main contributors

The report was prepared by staff of the Inclusive Labour Markets, Labour Relations and Working Conditions Branch (INWORK) of the ILO with contributions from other ILO colleagues in Geneva and in ILO field offices, under the responsibility of Philippe Marcadent, Chief of INWORK. Patrick Belser was the principal editor of the report. Rosalia Vazquez-Alvarez led the analysis for Part II of the report and coordinated inputs from consultants as well as the technical peer review. Kristen Sobeck updated the ILO Global Wage Database, produced the analyses for Part I and wrote Part I of the report. Research assistance was provided by Nicolas Maître. Chris Edgar and Charlotte Beauchamp coordinated the editing, publication and translation, and also handled the anonymous peer review of the report. Ksenija Radojevic Bovet was responsible for the proofreading. Christian Olsen designed the cover page. Inês Gomes designed several figures.

Sandra Polaski, ILO Deputy Director-General for Policy, provided strong guidance and support throughout the process, and contributed actively to the policy content of the report.

Specific contributions

Part II the report is based on a research project coordinated by Rosalia Vazquez-Alvarez. The project included data analysis and contributions from Roxana Maurizio (Universidad Nacional de General Sarmiento and CONICET, Argentina), Aico Peter Van Vuuren (University of Amsterdam), Ingrid Woolard (University of Cape Town), Youngjian Hu (Tianjin University of Finance and Economics, China), Li Shi and Wan Haiyuan (School of Economics and Management, Beijing Normal University, and Institute of Social Studies, National Development and Reform Commission, China) and Uma Rani (ILO Research Department). Marianne Furrer provided research assistance to Uma Rani for Part II of the report.

The technical peer review for Part II, carried out in addition to the general peer review of the report, was undertaken by Miguel Portela (Universidade do Minho, Braga, Portugal) and Andrea Regoli and Antonella D'Agostino (both of University of Naples "Parthenope"). Excerpts on the middle class and the motherhood pay gap were kindly contributed by, respectively, Alexandre Dormeier Freire (Graduate Institute of International and Development Studies, Geneva) and Damian Grimshaw and Jill Rubery (both of the University of Manchester Business School). Global and regional estimates in Part I of the report are based on the same methodology (described in Appendix I) as in earlier *Global Wage Reports*. This methodology was formulated by Malte Luebker (ILO Regional Office for Asia and the Pacific) in collaboration with Rafael Diez de Medina and Monica Castillo (both ILO, Department of Statistics) on the basis of a proposal by Farhad

Mehran (ILO consultant). The methodology was peer reviewed in 2011 by Yves Tillé (Institute of Statistics, University of Neuchâtel), Yujin Jeong (American University, Washington, DC), Joseph L. Gastwirth (George Washington University, Washington, DC) and Joyup Ahn (Korea Labor Institute).

Special thanks

Our special thanks go to Manuela Tomei, Director of the ILO's Conditions of Work and Equality Department, for her support and guidance. We also owe a special thanks to all the national statistical offices who assisted us with our data collection efforts.

We would further like to thank the entire team from ILO/SIALC (Information System and Labour Analysis) in Panama, in particular Bolívar Pino, for providing wage data on Latin America and the Caribbean, as well as Malte Luebker (ILO Regional Office for Asia and the Pacific) for sharing wage data from Asia and for providing new estimates of real wage growth in India. Special thanks are also due to Sangheon Lee (ILO, Geneva), who was part of the team of main contributors to previous editions of the report and who offered much guidance with this new edition. We also greatly appreciated the invaluable support we received from Edgardo Greising, Francisco Guerreiro and Marie-Claire Sodergren (ILO, Geneva) with respect to integrating the data used for this report into ILOSTAT. We would also like to thank Ekkehard Ernst, Salwa Haidar and Christian Viegelahn for providing data from ILO Global Employment Trends. Thanks also go to Najati Ghosheh for continuously pointing us to the most up-to-date academic literature.

We would also like to thank the following for their valuable input and comments: Laura Addati, Azita Berar Awad, Janine Berg, Duncan Campbell, Juan Chacaltana, Harvey Clavien, Rigoberto Garcia, David Glejberman, Susan Hayter, Richard Horne, James Howard, Martine Humblet, Iyanatul Islam, Samia Kazi Aoul, Michele Leighton, Nomaan Majid, Andres Marinakis, Adriana Mata-Greenwood, Jesse Mertens, Irmgard Nübler, Martin Oelz, Shauna Olney, Natalia Popova, Stephen Pursey, Wolfgang Scholz, Steven Tobin, Raymond Torres, Daniel Vaughan-Whitehead and the four anonymous peer reviewers.

Data sources

This report is based in part on data from Eurostat, EU-SILC, 2003 to 2010 inclusive, as well as on data from for the US PSID. The responsibility for all conclusions drawn from the data lies entirely with the authors.

Executive summary

Part I. Major trends in wages

The context

Debates about the economic role of wages have intensified in recent years. At the firm level, an increase or decrease in wages affects production costs and has consequences for profitability, sustainability and competitiveness. At the country level, the net effect of higher or lower wages depends on the direction and relative magnitude of the effects of wages on household consumption, investment and net exports. In the Eurozone, concerns over deficits in aggregate demand arising from insufficient household consumption have focused more attention on wages, and many commentators have pointed to the decline or stagnation of wages as increasing the risk of deflation. In some emerging and developing economies, more attention has been devoted to wages as a key component of overall strategies to reduce poverty and inequality.

Global wage growth decelerated in 2013 compared to 2012, and has yet to rebound to pre-crisis rates

Global real wage growth dropped sharply during the crisis in 2008 and 2009, recovered somewhat in 2010 and then decelerated again. Average monthly real wages grew globally by 2.0 per cent in 2013, down from 2.2 per cent in 2012, and have yet to rebound to pre-crisis rates of around 3.0 per cent growth in 2006 and 2007.

Global wage growth driven mostly by emerging and developing economies

Global wage growth in recent years was driven by emerging and developing economies, where real wages have been rising – sometimes rapidly – since 2007. However, there are major regional variations. While real wage growth in 2013 reached 6 per cent in Asia and nearly 6 per cent in Eastern Europe and Central Asia, it amounted to less than 1 per cent in Latin America and the Caribbean (down from 2.3 per cent in 2012). Tentative estimates also show that real wages grew by almost 4 per cent in the Middle East, due to strong reported wage growth in Saudi Arabia, but by less than 1 per cent in Africa. Real wage growth in emerging G20 economies slowed from 6.7 per cent in 2012 to 5.9 per cent in 2013.

Global wage growth cut in half when China is excluded

China accounted for much of global wage growth, because of its large size and high real wage growth. Excluding China cuts global real wage growth almost in half, from 2.0 per cent to 1.1 per cent in 2013, and from 2.2 per cent to 1.3 per cent in 2012.

Flat wages in developed economies

In the group of developed economies, real wages were flat in 2012 and 2013, growing by 0.1 per cent and 0.2 per cent, respectively. In some cases – including Greece, Ireland, Italy, Japan, Spain and the United Kingdom – average real wages in 2013 were below their 2007 level. Composition effects (the effect on the average wage due to the changing composition of workers in paid employment) played a large role in crisis-affected countries.

Between 1999 and 2013, labour productivity growth in developed economies outstripped real wage growth, and labour's share of national income – also a reflection of the link between wages and productivity – fell in the largest developed economies

Overall, in the group of developed economies, real wage growth lagged behind labour productivity growth over the period 1999 to 2013. This was the case before the crisis in 2007 and – after a brief narrowing of the gap during the depth of the crisis – labour productivity has continued to outstrip real wage growth since 2009.

Between 1999 and 2013, labour productivity growth exceeded wage growth in Germany, Japan and the United States. This decoupling of wages and productivity growth is reflected in the decline in the labour income share (the share of GDP going to labour compensation) over the same period in these countries. In other countries, such as France and the United Kingdom, the labour income share remained stable or increased. Among emerging economies, the labour income share increased in recent years in the Russian Federation, and declined in China, Mexico and Turkey. It is important to note, however, that when real wage growth is rapid, the welfare implications of a declining labour income share in emerging and developing economies may be different from those in developed economies.

Average wages in emerging and developing economies are slowly converging towards average wages in developed economies

Average wages are still considerably lower in emerging and developing economies than they are in most developed economies. When measured in purchasing power parity (PPP), the average monthly wage in the United States, for example, is more than triple that in China.

While definitional and methodological differences make precise comparison of wage levels across countries difficult, the average wage in developed economies is estimated at approximately US$ (PPP) 3,000, as compared to an average wage in emerging and developing economies of about US$ (PPP) 1,000. The estimated world average monthly wage is about US$ (PPP) 1,600. However, the gap in real wages between developed and emerging economies has narrowed between 2000 and 2012, based on strong wage growth in the latter, while in many developed countries wages stagnated or contracted.

Part II. Wages and income inequality

Mixed trends in household income inequality

Growing inequality in many countries over the last few decades has commanded increasing attention, as high levels of inequality can adversely affect well-being and social cohesion as well as reducing medium- and long-term economic growth. The report shows that recent trends in total household income inequality have been mixed in both developed economies and emerging and developing economies. The level of inequality is generally higher in the latter; however, progress has been made in a number of such countries to reduce it, usually in a context of growing incomes. In developed economies that experienced rising inequality, this has typically occurred in a context of stagnant or declining incomes.

Inequality starts in the labour market

In many countries, inequality starts in the labour market. Changes in the distribution of wages and paid employment have been key factors behind recent inequality trends. In developed economies where inequality increased most, this was frequently due to a combination of more wage inequality and job losses. In Spain and the United States, the two countries where this inequality between the top and bottom 10 per cent increased most, changes in the distribution of wages and job losses accounted for 90 per cent of the increase in inequality in Spain and 140 per cent of the increase in the United States. In developed countries where household income inequality increased, other income sources offset about one-third of the increase in inequality due to changes in wages and employment.

A number of emerging and developing economies experienced declines in inequality. In these countries, a more equitable distribution of wages and paid employment was a predominant factor. In Argentina and Brazil, where inequality fell most, changes in the distribution of wages and paid employment accounted for 87 per cent of the decade-long reduction in top–bottom inequality in Argentina, as they did for 72 per cent in Brazil.

Wages are a major source of household income

The important role of wages in household income inequality can be explained by the fact that wages are a major source of household income in both developed economies and emerging and developing economies. In developed economies, wages represent about 70 to 80 per cent of total pre-tax, post-transfers income for households with at least one member of working age, with substantial variation across countries. In the emerging and developing economies studied in the report, the contribution of wages to household income is smaller, ranging from about 50 to 60 per cent in Argentina and Brazil to about 40 per cent in Peru and 30 per cent in Viet Nam. Self-employment income generally comprises a larger share of household income than in developed economies, particularly among low-income groups.

However, in both types of economies, income sources at both the top and the bottom are more diverse than in the middle, where households rely mostly on wages. In developed economies, social transfers play an important role in supporting low-income households, whereas in many emerging and developing economies low-income households rely mostly on self-employment. Among the bottom 10 per cent of households, for example, wages represent roughly 50 per cent of household income in the United States, 30 per cent in Italy, 25 per cent in France, 20 per cent in the United Kingdom, 10 per cent in Germany and 5 per cent in Romania. Among the middle- and upper-income groups, wages represent the highest share of household income in almost all countries, reaching about 80 per cent or more in Germany, the United Kingdom and the United States.

For emerging and developing countries, the share of wages among the bottom 10 per cent of households varies from about 50 per cent of household income in the Russian Federation to less than 10 per cent in Viet Nam. In Argentina, Brazil, China and the Russian Federation, the share of wages rises gradually across the middle classes, before declining in the highest income groups.

Some groups suffer from discrimination and wage penalties

The report shows that in almost all countries studied there are wage gaps between men and women as well as between national and migrant workers. These gaps arise for multiple and complex reasons that differ from one country to another and vary at different points of the overall wage distribution. These wage gaps can be divided into an "explained" part, which is accounted for by observed human capital and labour market characteristics, and an "unexplained" part, which captures wage discrimination and includes characteristics (e.g. having children) that should in principle have no effect on wages. The report shows that if this unexplained wage penalty was eliminated, the mean gender wage gap would actually reverse in Brazil, Lithuania, the Russian Federation, Slovenia and Sweden, where the labour market characteristics of the disadvantaged groups should result in higher wages. It would also nearly disappear in about half the countries in the sample of developed economies.

A similar analysis is carried out to compare the wages of migrants with those of national workers, showing that in various countries the mean wage gap would reverse if the unexplained part of the gap was eliminated. Among developed economies, this is the case in Denmark, Germany, Luxembourg, the Netherlands, Norway, Poland and Sweden. In Chile, migrant workers earn more than their national counterparts on average.

The report also finds a wage gap between workers in the formal and the informal economy; this is shown in the report, for example, in wage gaps affecting workers in the informal economy for selected Latin American countries. As with gender and migrant wage gaps, the wage gap for workers in the informal economy is generally lowest in the bottom deciles and increases for higher wage earners. In addition, the observable labour market characteristics of informal economy workers differ from workers in the formal economy across all points of the wage distribution and for all countries (i.e. there is an explained gap across the entire distribution). At the same time, however, the unexplained part of the wage gap remains significant.

Part III. Policy responses to address wages and inequality

The policy challenge

Inequality can be addressed through policies that affect wage distribution directly or indirectly and through fiscal policies that redistribute income through taxation and transfers. However, increasing inequality in the labour market places a heavier burden on efforts to reduce inequality through taxes and transfers, which is not always possible or desirable. This suggests that inequality that arises within the labour market should also be addressed through policies that have a direct effect on the distribution of wages.

Minimum wages and collective bargaining

Recent research suggests that governments have considerable space for using minimum wages as a policy tool. On the one hand, research shows that there is either no trade-off between increased minimum wages and employment levels or that such increases have very limited effects on employment, which can be either positive or negative. On the other, it shows that minimum wages do contribute effectively to reducing wage inequality. Minimum wage policies have been used as effective policy tools by an increasing number of governments in recent years, in both developed economies and emerging and developing economies. Importantly, minimum wages should be set in a way that balances the needs of workers and their families with economic factors.

Collective bargaining is another labour market institution that has long been recognized as a key instrument for addressing inequality in general and wage inequality in particular. The extent to which collective bargaining can compress overall wage inequality depends on the proportion of workers covered by collective agreements and on the position of these workers in the wage distribution.

Promoting job creation

Job creation is a priority in all countries, and the report shows that access to, or loss of, paid employment is a key determinant of income inequality. In developed economies, job losses that disproportionally affected low-income workers contributed to increasing inequality. In emerging and developing economies, the creation of paid employment for those at the bottom contributed to reducing inequality in a number of countries. These findings confirm that the pursuit of full-employment policies is an important aspect of reducing inequality. The promotion of sustainable enterprises is key in this regard. This involves establishing an environment favourable to the creation and development of enterprises, as well as to innovation and enhanced productivity. The resulting benefits can be shared equitably within enterprises and in society more broadly.

Special attention to disadvantaged groups of workers

Extending minimum wages and collective bargaining to low-paid workers will generally be helpful in reducing inequality among women, migrants and vulnerable groups, who are over-represented among these workers. However, these policy tools alone will not eliminate all forms of discrimination or wage gaps, which constitute a significant source of inequality. A wider range of policies is required to overcome wage gaps across groups that are not explained by human capital and labour market characteristics. For example, achieving equal pay between men and women requires policies aimed at combating discriminatory practices and gender-based stereotypes about the value of women's work, effective policies on maternity, paternity and parental leave, as well as advocacy for better sharing of family responsibilities.

Fiscal redistribution through taxes and social protection systems

Fiscal policies can compensate to some extent for inequality in the labour market, through both progressive taxation systems and transfers that tend to equalize household incomes. Such policies are used more frequently by governments in developed economies to address their income distribution objectives than in emerging and developing economies, although there may be some convergence under way. In emerging and developing economies, there appears to be space for increased tax revenues through a variety of measures, including by broadening the tax base through the transition of workers and enterprises from the informal to the formal economy as well as by improving tax collection. Increased revenues would in turn allow for the extension and upgrading of social protection systems, which are often not fully developed in such economies.

The need for combined policy action

Wages constitute the largest single source of income for households in developed and emerging economies alike, with only a few exceptions. At the same time, wages make a smaller contribution to household income for the lowest income groups. In developed economies, where social transfers are more important sources of income for these groups, this calls for a combination of policies that help individuals in these households move into employment and measures that raise the quality and compensation of the work they find. In some emerging and developing economies, raising the income of low-income groups has been achieved through direct employment programmes (as in India and South Africa) and cash transfers (as in Brazil and Mexico, among many other countries). In the end, the most effective and sustainable route out of poverty for the working-age population is a productive, fairly paid job. Policies should be geared towards this objective.

PART I Major trends in wages

1 Introduction

Debates about the economic role of wages in the global recovery have intensified since the publication of the last edition of the ILO *Global Wage Report* (ILO, 2012a). At the firm level, wages represent a motivating factor for workers, but also a cost to enterprises. At the country level, however, the sum of all enterprise-level wage adjustments can have complex effects. Since wages represent an important source of household income, lower wages tend to reduce household consumption, thereby depressing aggregate demand, unless that negative effect is offset by substantial gains in investment and net exports. The net effect of higher or lower wages on aggregate demand thus depends on the direction and relative magnitude of the effects of wages on its different components, including household consumption, investment and net exports.[1]

This macroeconomic perspective is not new, but after virtually disappearing from policy debates, it has received new attention in recent years, as many countries seek to achieve positive growth rates and create jobs while at the same time trying to reduce imbalances between their imports and their exports. Wage policies and wage trends play an important role in this equation. In countries with large current account deficits, where imports exceed exports, wage moderation may contribute to rebalancing trade accounts. This can have a positive effect on aggregate demand and employment if the boost to the competitiveness of exports is large. However, if wage cuts reduce domestic consumption by more than is offset by an increase in exports, the result will be negative in terms of GDP growth, particularly if government spending is reduced at the same time. In countries with large trade surpluses, higher wage growth can contribute to a rebalancing of demand towards domestic household consumption and away from exports – with the effect on aggregate demand in these countries again depending on the magnitude of the different elements of demand.

At the international level, a lack of policy coordination incurs risks. If too many countries with close economic ties or in a large geographical area (such as the European Union) simultaneously pursue a policy of "wage moderation", the result is likely to be a shortfall in aggregate demand and a reliance on consumers in other regions. As the previous *Global Wage Report* (ILO, 2012a) has pointed out, in the years before the global economic and financial crisis, wages failed to increase in line with labour productivity in many countries, particularly – but not only – in some of the large developed economies. The growing gap between wages and productivity has translated into a declining labour income share in these countries (see EC, 2007; Guerriero, 2012; ILO, 2008a; IMF, 2007; Karabarbounis and

Neiman, 2014), and may have contributed to structurally weak aggregate demand in the years before the crisis (Wolf, 2014a).

In response, policies have started to shift. China, Germany, Japan and the United States, for example, have recently introduced measures likely to boost wage growth. Amongst these policy shifts, Germany has adopted a new minimum wage which will come into effect in 2015, and Japan has encouraged its companies to increase basic pay. Such policy shifts have been supported by IMF recommendations.[2] In China, authorities are seeking to rebalance the economy towards more domestic consumption. Meanwhile, the United States, which has long experienced consumption sustained by credit more than wage growth, is also seeking to encourage real wage growth to "make up for a decades-long trend of average wages failing to keep pace with productivity gains" (USCEA, 2014, pp. 36–37).[3] The IMF noted that "wages are stagnant" in the United States and called for an increase in the minimum wage, combined with an expansion of the earned income tax credit (EITC), both to reduce poverty levels and to provide some support to aggregate demand (IMF, 2014a; Bloomberg, 2014).

In other countries, wage moderation (or even wage cuts) was seen as part of a set of necessary adjustments to improve competitiveness and sustain employment levels during the crisis. For example, the Bank of England considered that in the United Kingdom a rising unemployment rate was prevented by wage moderation.[4] European countries most affected by the sovereign debt crisis have also experienced wage cuts. While these wage adjustments may have contributed to fostering external competitiveness, their effects on aggregate demand – combined with those of fiscal consolidation[5] – have turned out to be more adverse than expected, and further wage cuts in those countries are likely to be counterproductive (OECD, 2014b).

At the global policy level, the G20 ministers of finance and the ministers of labour and employment called for the creation of "better jobs" (G20, 2014a, paras 12–17) and for "policies to reinforce the links between productivity, wages and employment" (G20, 2013a, para. 8.5).

It is within this global context that Part I of this report presents the latest trends in average wages.

2 Trends in average wage growth in the global economy

Wage trends take place within the broader macroeconomic context and the different experiences of developed economies and emerging and developing economies. The global economy contracted sharply between 2007 and 2009, quickly recovered in 2010, but subsequently decelerated (figure 1). While growth rates after 2010 declined across the globe, they remained much higher in emerging and developing economies than in advanced economies. Several ILO reports[6] have pointed out that labour markets are still in a state of disarray in many countries, and that the global jobs deficit is worse today than before the onset of the global financial and economic crisis in 2008. The challenge of absorbing the estimated 199.4 million unemployed and integrating the 395.7 million new entrants into the labour market in the next decade is enormous.

How have recent economic trends been reflected in average real wages? Figure 2 provides two estimates (for a definition of wages, see box 1). The first is a global estimate based on wage data for 130 economies using the methodology described in Appendix I and the Global Wage Database (see box 2). The second is also a global estimate, but omits China because of its large size (in terms of number of wage earners) and high real wage growth, which remained in double digits for most of the 2000s and accounted for much of the global wage growth. As can be seen from figure 2, global real wage growth dropped sharply during the crisis in 2008 and 2009, recovered somewhat in 2010 and then decelerated again. It has yet to rebound to its pre-crisis rates.

Figure 3 shows estimates for the G20 as a whole and for its developed as well as its emerging members.[7] Together, the countries of the G20 produce about three-quarters of world GDP[8] and employ more than 1 billion of the world's 1.5 billion paid employees.[9] Average real wage growth throughout the period

Figure 1 Annual average economic growth, 1995–2013 (GDP in constant prices)

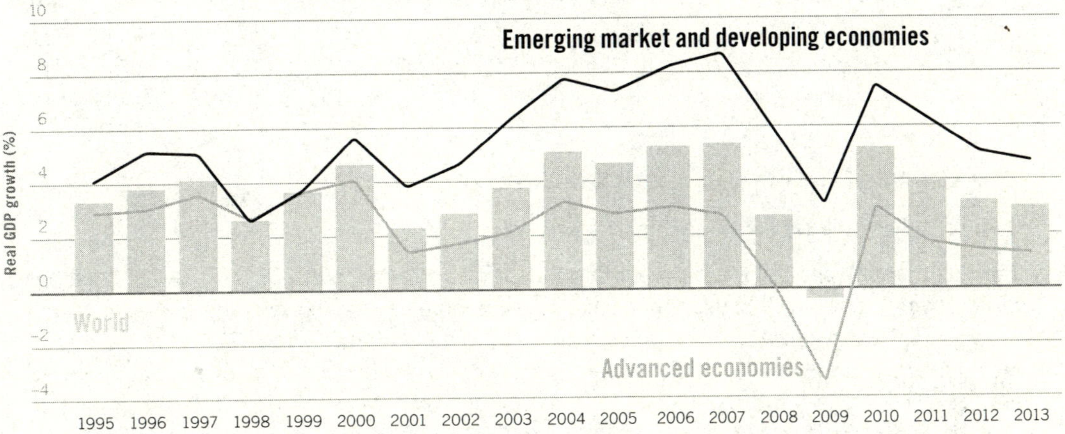

Note: Country groups are those used by the IMF as described in the appendix of the IMF's *World Economic Outlook*, Apr. 2014.
Source: IMF, *World Economic Outlook* database, Apr. 2014. Data accessible at: www.ilo.org/gwr-figures

was driven by emerging and developing economies; the same pattern emerges from the regional figures presented in figure 12 below. By contrast, in G20 developed economies average real wage growth remained low or negative throughout the period.

Average wages are calculated using gross monthly wages (where available), rather than the less frequently available hourly wages, and fluctuations therefore reflect changes in both hourly wages and the average number of hours worked; they are also net of consumer price inflation (i.e. deflated by the consumer price index or CPI).[10]

Box 1 What are wages?

Wherever possible, in this report wages are defined according to the ILO definition of earnings adopted by the 12th International Conference of Labour Statisticians (ILO, 1973).

(1) Direct wages and salaries for time worked, or work done, cover: (i) straight-time pay of time-rated workers; (ii) incentive pay of time-rated workers; (iii) earnings of piece-workers (excluding overtime premiums); (iv) premium pay for overtime, shift, night and holiday work; and (v) commissions paid to sales and other personnel. Included are: premiums for seniority and special skills; geographical zone differentials; responsibility premiums; dirt, danger and discomfort allowances; payments under guaranteed wage systems; cost-of-living allowances; and other allowances.

(2) Remuneration for time not worked comprises: direct payments to employees in respect of public holidays, annual vacations, and other time off with pay granted by the employer.

(3) Bonuses and gratuities cover: seasonal and end-of-year bonuses; additional payments in respect of vacation periods (supplementary to normal pay); and profit-sharing bonuses.

Earnings include cash earnings and in-kind payments, but the two should be distinguished from each other.

There are also related concepts which are broader. For example, while one element of labour cost is earnings, it also includes other elements such as: food, drink, fuel and other payments in kind, cost of workers' housing borne by employers; employers' social security expenditure; cost of vocational training; cost of welfare services (e.g. canteen, recreational facilities); labour costs not classified elsewhere (e.g. cost of work clothes), and taxes regarded as labour cost (e.g. taxes on employment or payrolls). For a detailed description of these elements, see ILO, 1966.

Source: ILO, 1973.

Box 2 The ILO Global Wage Database

Data underlying the *Global Wage Report* are accessible at: www.ilo.org/ilostat/GWR

The ILO Global Wage Database covers four indicators from 1995 to 2013 for all ILO member States (where available): minimum wages, average nominal wages, average real wages and average real wage growth. In previous years, the data underlying the *Global Wage Report* included many additional indicators (e.g. low pay, wage inequality by decile, wages by sex, etc.). However, since the publication of the *Global Wage Report 2012/13*, the compilation of these indicators has been transferred to the "Yearly indicators" collection of ILOSTAT at: http://www.ilo.org/ilostat).

Figure 2 Annual average global real wage growth, 2006–13

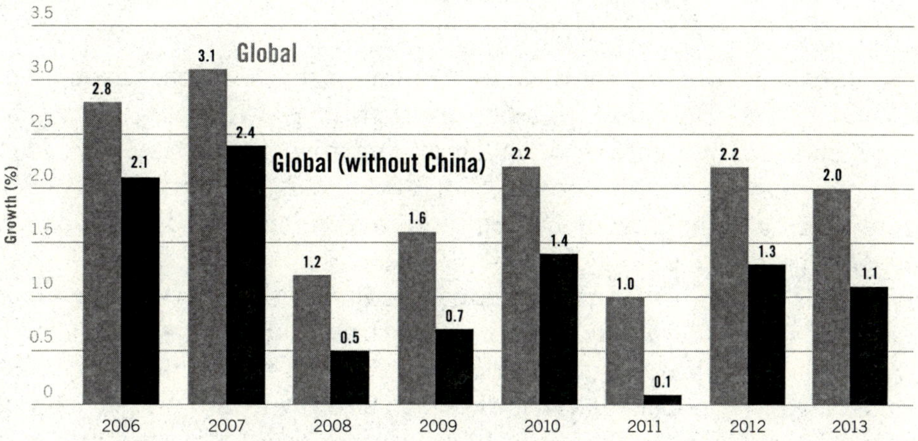

Note: Global wage growth is calculated as a weighted average of year-on-year growth in average monthly real wages in 130 countries, covering 95.8 per cent of all employees in the world (for a description of the methodology, see Appendix I).

Source: ILO Global Wage Database. Data accessible at: www.ilo.org/gwr-figures

Figure 3 Annual average real wage growth in the G20, 2006–13

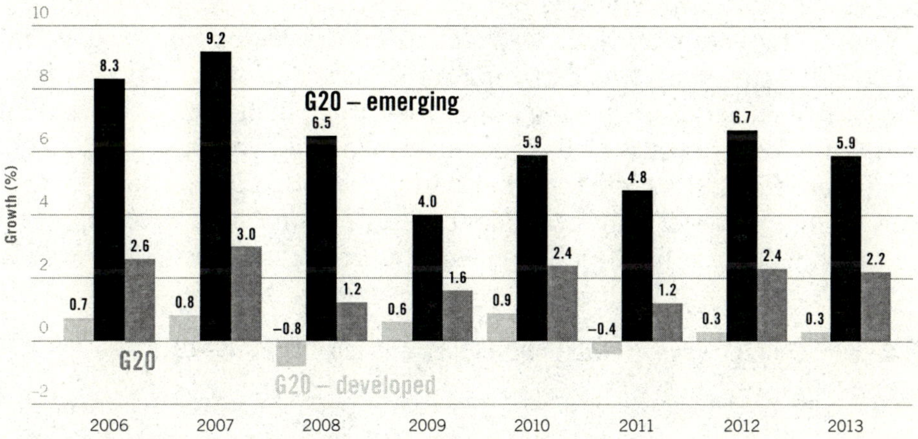

Note: The estimate for the G20 uses the methodology specified in Appendix I, but is restricted to 18 out of 19 individual countries for which data are available (Argentina identified some inconsistencies in its wage series for some years and has been excluded).

Source: ILO Global Wage Database. Data accessible at: www.ilo.org/gwr-figures

3 Developed economies

3.1 Average wages: Some variation across countries

Looking at developed economies (for the composition of this and other groupings used, see Appendix I), it is apparent from figure 4 that the growth rates of average real wages have tended to fluctuate within a low and narrow range since 2006. This pattern has become particularly pronounced in 2012 and 2013, years of virtually flat wages, contributing in the current low inflation environment to concerns about possible risks of deflation.

Figure 5 looks at the individual developed economy members in the G20, which represent the largest developed economies in the world. It shows the variety that exists within the overall trend depicted in figure 4. In France and the United States, average wages are consistent with the pattern shown in figure 4, having been relatively stagnant, with only minor fluctuations. However, Australia and Canada show more positive growth in average wages partially attributed by some to their natural-resource based growth during a boom in commodities (Downes, Hanslow and Tulip, 2014; Statistics Canada, 2014). Conversely, notable declines are observed in Italy and the United Kingdom, where the deep recession was accompanied by an unprecedented period of falling real wages. According to the Low Pay Commission, British wages fell more sharply than at any time since records began in 1964 (Low Pay Commission, 2014).

Figure 6 shows the extent to which wages changed in selected European countries most affected by the crisis. Most striking is the large decline in Greek wages, resulting in part from a series of specific policy measures, including a 22 per cent cut in the minimum wage for unskilled workers aged 25 and over and a 32 per cent cut for those under 25 in 2012. Collective bargaining was also decentralized, with priority given to enterprise-level agreements in cases of conflict with higher-level agreements, which tended to facilitate downward wage adjustments (ILO, 2014a).

Figure 4 Annual average real wage growth in developed economies, 2006–13

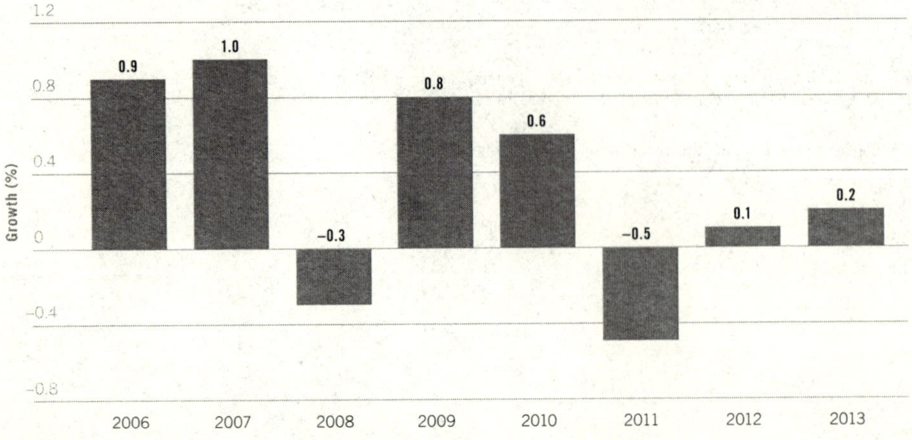

Note: Wage growth is calculated as a weighted average of year-on-year growth in average monthly real wages in 36 countries (for a description of the methodology, see Appendix I).

Source: ILO Global Wage Database. Data accessible at: www.ilo.org/gwr-figures

Figure 5 Average real wage index for developed G20 countries, 2007–13

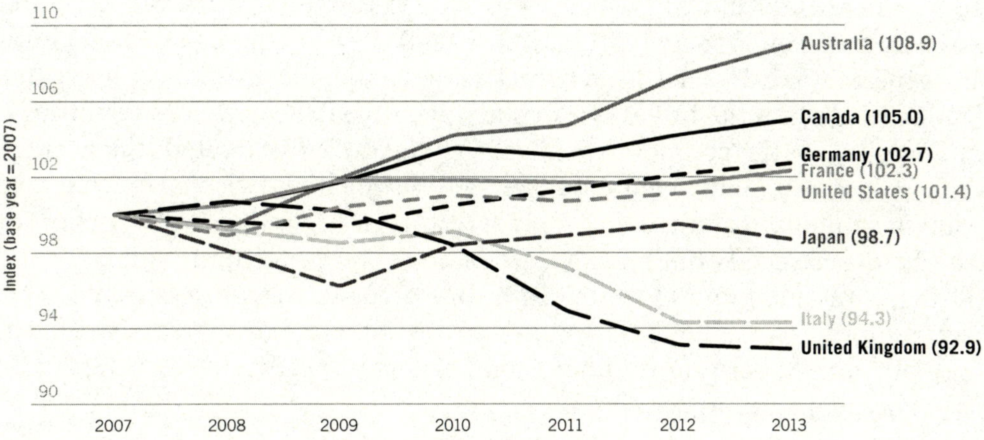

Source: ILO Global Wage Database. Data accessible at: www.ilo.org/gwr-figures

Figure 6 Average real wage index for selected European countries most affected by the crisis, 2007–13

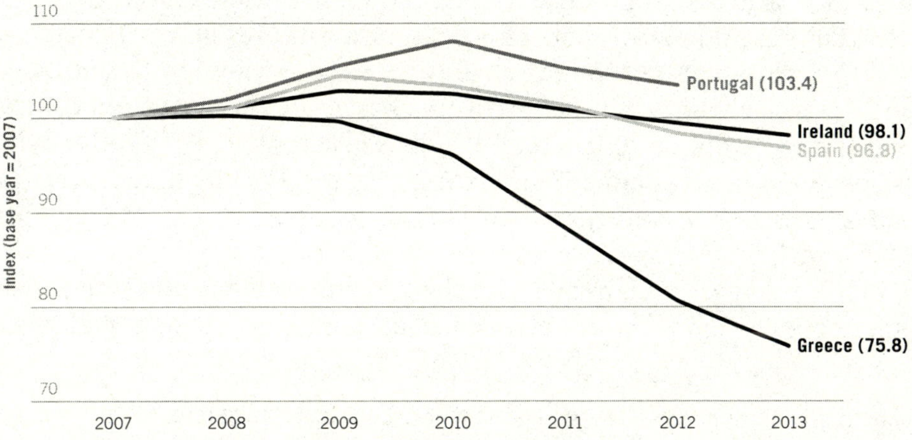

Source: ILO Global Wage Database. Data accessible at: www.ilo.org/gwr-figures

Box 3 The composition effect

Average real wages change from year to year not only when the wages of employees increase or decrease over time, but also when the composition of the labour force changes. For example, if low-paid employees are the first to be dismissed in a recession, the average wage of the remaining employees who are employed automatically increases. Conversely, if newly hired employees are paid less than others, then the average wage automatically decreases. This so-called *composition effect* creates a countercyclical bias in the data (understating wage growth in upswings, but also understating wage declines in downturns), which has at times contributed to a perception that real wages tend to be "inflexible". However, some research with panel data (tracking only the wages of individuals who remain employed) reveals that real wages generally adjust much more substantially than had been thought during economic ups and downs (see e.g. Martins, Solon and Thomas, 2012; Abraham and Haltiwanger, 1995; Solon, Barsky and Parker, 1994).

Public sector wages were further reduced several times during the crisis, contributing to a 23 per cent decline in government expenditure related to compensation of employees between 2008 and 2012 (ILO, 2014a). In other crisis-affected countries, the general wage declines have been less dramatic, but the focus on average wages tends to obscure the full extent of the wage turbulence in these countries.

In Spain, when the composition effect (see box 3) is discounted, the average wages of those who remained employed seem to have fallen twice as much as the trend shown in figure 6 (Banco de España, 2014). In Ireland, the proportion of workers who experienced nominal pay cuts exceeded 50 per cent in both 2009 and 2010 (Doris, Sweetman and O'Neill, 2013). In Portugal, the wages of civil servants earning more than €1,500 per month and of blue-collar workers were cut, and those of some 40 per cent of other wage earners were frozen (see ILO, 2013b; Carneiro, Portugal and Varejao, 2013).

3.2 Productivity outstrips wage growth

Are differences in wage trends across countries a product of differences in labour productivity growth? Figure 7 shows the relationship between wages and productivity from 1999 to 2013 in the group of developed economies where labour productivity refers to GDP (output) per worker. This definition captures how productively labour is used to generate output, but also captures the contribution to output of other elements such as changes in hours worked, changes in the skill composition of labour, and the contribution of capital.[11] While other measures of productivity exist, labour productivity as defined here is used by the ILO as a decent work indicator, and is the only one readily available for all countries up to and including 2013.[12]

Figure 7 shows that after a narrowing of the gap during the depth of the crisis between 2008 and 2009, labour productivity has continued to outstrip real wage

Figure 7 Trends in growth in average wages and labour productivity in developed economies (index), 1999–2013

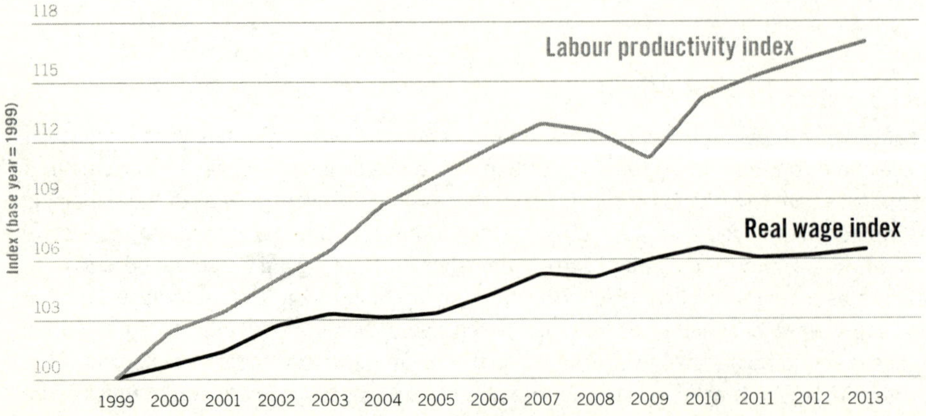

Note: Wage growth is calculated as a weighted average of year-on-year growth in average monthly real wages in 36 economies (for a description of the methodology, see Appendix I). Index is based to 1999 because of data availability.

Sources: ILO Global Wage Database; ILO *Trends Econometric Models*, Apr. 2014. Data accessible at: www.ilo.org/gwr-figures

Box 4 The relationship between wages, compensation, different deflators and labour productivity

Since wages represent only one component of labour costs (see box 1), it may be more appropriate to compare gains in labour productivity with increases in average compensation per employee (as opposed to wages). Compensation of employees includes wages and salaries payable in cash or in kind *and* social insurance contributions payable by employers (CEC, IMF, OECD, UN and World Bank, 2009, para. 7.42).* To address this argument, figure 8 compares the change in labour productivity with the changes in average real wages and in average real compensation per employee; as can be seen, the gap still persists.

A second area of debate surrounds the most appropriate tool to be used to deflate wages or labour compensation: the consumer price index (CPI) or the GDP deflator. The GDP deflator captures the change in prices of all goods and services produced in the economy. In contrast, the CPI reflects the prices which affect consumers (i.e. the prices of goods and services consumers buy). Thus, the GDP deflator and the CPI can differ, because the overall price of the basket of goods bought by consumers is different from the overall price of all goods produced domestically. So which deflator is more appropriate in calculating changes in real wages and/or labour compensation? It depends on the end-use of the analysis. When the standard of living is being assessed, the CPI more accurately reflects changes in the purchasing power of consumers: this is why the *Global Wage Report* uses the CPI to calculate its global and regional estimates for average real wage growth. However, for enterprises, the relevant measure may be between productivity and labour compensation deflated by the product price; in this case, the GDP deflator may be more appropriate (Feldstein, 2008).

To address this second issue, two additional calculations are presented in figure 8, which compares labour productivity growth with real compensation per employee deflated by both the CPI and the GDP deflator. The results show that, just as in the case of the concept of wages/compensation used, it is likewise with the different deflators; whichever is used, a gap remains.

A detailed study by the US Bureau of Labor Statistics corroborates this finding for the United States: it shows that while these measurement issues do affect the exact estimates, they do not affect the overall conclusion that productivity grew faster than wages (Fleck, Glaser and Sprague, 2011). There was also a similar finding for the United States in 2014 in the *Economic report of the President* (USCEA, 2014).

* By definition, compensation of employees omits the income of the self-employed. To calculate the adjusted wage share, there are several methods. See ILO, 2010a, Technical Appendix II.

Figure 8 Labour productivity, real wages and estimated real compensation per employee in developed economies (indices), 1999–2013

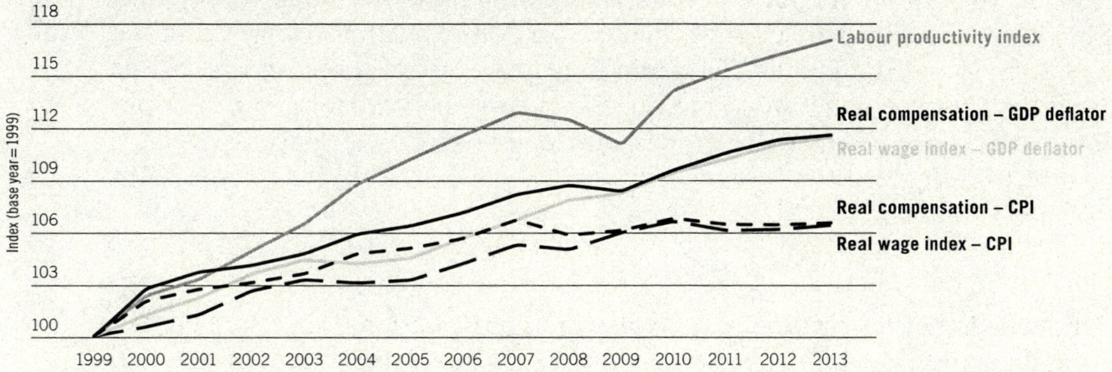

Note: Wage growth is calculated as a weighted average of year-on-year growth in average monthly real wages in 33 economies (for a description of the methodology, see Appendix I). Iceland, Israel and Malta were excluded from this figure for reasons of data availability; these three countries collectively contribute less than 1 per cent of the total employees in developed economies. Index is based to 1999 because of data availability.

Sources: ILO Global Wage Database; ILO *Trends Econometric Models*, Apr. 2014; IMF, *World Economic Outlook*, Apr. 2014; European Commission AMECO database. Data accessible at: www.ilo.org/gwr-figures

Figure 9 Estimated real labour compensation per employee and labour productivity growth in the largest developed economies, deflated by the CPI and GDP deflator, 1999–2013

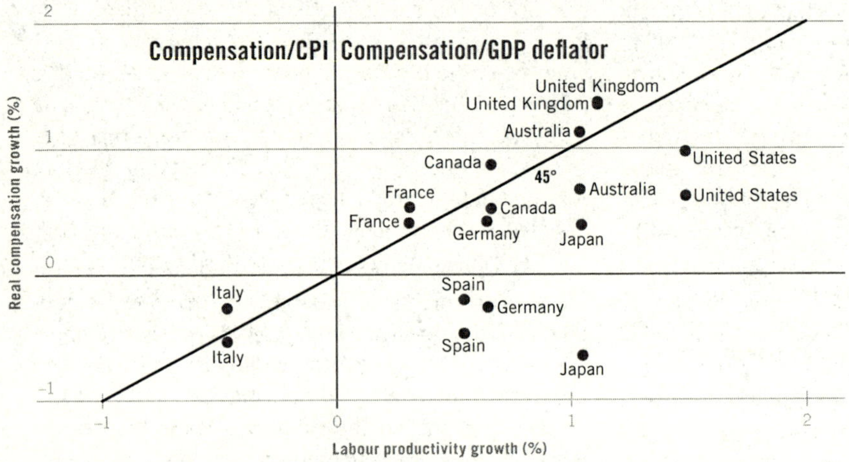

Sources: European Commission AMECO database; IMF, *World Economic Outlook*, Apr. 2014; ILO *Trends Econometric Models*, Apr. 2014. Data accessible at: www.ilo.org/gwr-figures

growth in this group of countries. Even when changes in real wages are calculated using not the CPI but the GDP deflator, the trend presented in figure 7 persists (see box 4).

The overall picture for developed economies is strongly influenced by the largest economies in the group, in particular Germany, Japan and the United States. Figure 9 shows the relationship between productivity and real compensation per employee (as opposed to real wages) for selected developed economies between 1999 and 2013, using both the CPI and the GDP deflator. Real labour compensation per employee is used instead of wages since it is more closely linked to trends in the labour income share (see section 3.3 below). In several countries, labour productivity grew faster than labour compensation. However, in the cases of France and the United Kingdom they grew fairly closely in line, while in Australia, Canada and Italy the relationship between real compensation per employee and labour productivity growth, during this particular period, depends on the deflator used.[13]

3.3 Labour income shares

The labour income share measures the distribution of national income between labour and capital; when it declines, this implies that a smaller share of national income is going to workers. As pointed out in the Introduction, a considerable number of studies have documented the decline in the labour share in many developed economies since the 1980s. This decline happened in part because of a shift in employment from labour-intensive to more capital-intensive sectors. But the larger part of the trend since the 1990s is explained by the fall of the labour income share within industries, particularly in high- and medium-technology manufacturing, and in financial services where profits soared.[14] The available literature suggests that this may have been due to a combination of pressure from financial markets for high capital returns, globalization of international trade, technological change and the simultaneous erosion of the redistributive power of labour market institutions (ILO, 2012a). Under most circumstances, a decline in the labour share reflects a situation where labour productivity is growing faster than average wages. The potential macroeconomic consequences of a continued decline in the labour income share can be significant, including the constraining effect on household income and consumption, which can contribute to the stagnation of aggregate demand and undermine firms' incentives to invest due to uncertain future sources of demand, as recently highlighted in the joint ILO/OECD/World Bank report to the G20 (ILO, OECD and World Bank, 2014).

Figure 10 shows how the labour income share has changed since 1991 in the developed G20 countries. The unadjusted labour income only includes compensation of employees, whereas the adjusted labour income share used in figure 10 makes an adjustment to account for the self-employed as well.[15] In Canada (and also in Australia), part of the decline is tied to the rise in commodity prices; profits in the mining, oil and gas sectors in Canada doubled between 2000 and 2006 (Sharpe, Arsenault and Harrison, 2008; Rao, Sharpe and Smith, 2005). In Japan, the decline is attributable in part to labour market reforms in the mid-1990s, when more industries were allowed to hire non-regular workers; the consequent influx of non-regular workers, who often earned less than regular workers, contributed to the stagnation of wages over time (Sommer, 2009; Agnese and Sala, 2011). In France, the labour income share remained relatively stable. In Italy and the United Kingdom, the trend is unclear: while the labour income share declined in the early part of the 1990s, since then wages and productivity have grown at a similar pace. In the United Kingdom, the Low Pay Commission has estimated that employees'

Figure 10 Adjusted labour income share in developed G20 countries, 1991–2013

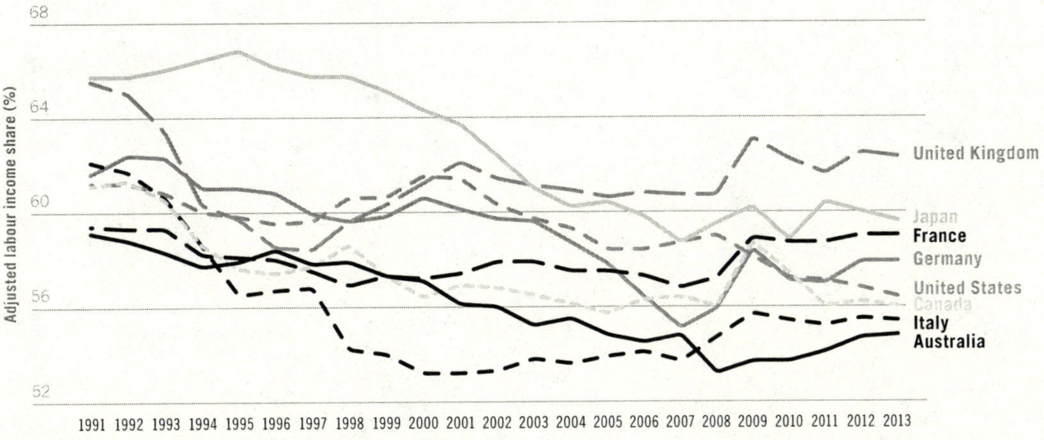

Note: Adjusted wage share, total economy, as a percentage of GDP at current market prices (compensation per employee as a percentage of GDP at market prices per person employed).

Source: European Commission AMECO database. Data accessible at: www.ilo.org/gwr-figures

Figure 11 Adjusted labour income share in selected European countries most affected by the crisis, 1991–2013

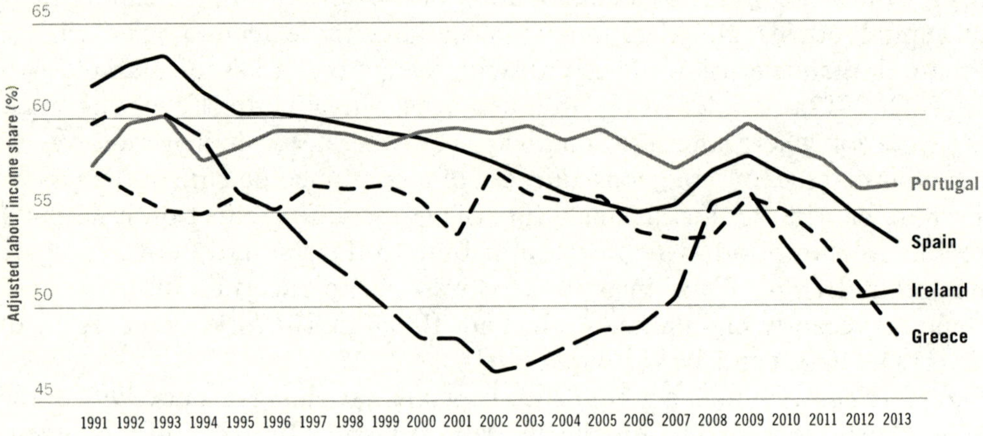

Note: Adjusted wage share, total economy, as a percentage of GDP at current market prices (compensation per employee as a percentage of GDP at market prices per person employed).

Source: European Commission AMECO database. Data accessible at: www.ilo.org/gwr-figures

compensation and productivity have grown at more or less the same rate since 1964 (Low Pay Commission, 2014). In Italy, one factor contributing to the decline in the labour income share at the beginning of the 1990s was a set of labour market reforms that changed the wage bargaining system to curb wage growth (Lucidi and Kleinknecht, 2010). In Germany, after years of wage moderation, the labour income share has partly recovered in recent years.

Turning to European countries most affected by the crisis, figure 11 points to the large decline in the Greek labour income share, to the sharp reversals of wage shares in the Irish labour market, and to the continuously falling labour income share in Spain since 2009.

4 Trends in emerging and developing economies

4.1 Higher wage growth

In many emerging and developing economies, average real wages have tended to increase more rapidly than in developed economies. Figure 12 presents the annual average real wage growth by region, showing rates that are higher than those of developed economies in most years.

Figure 12 Average real wage growth in emerging and developing economies, by region, 2006–13

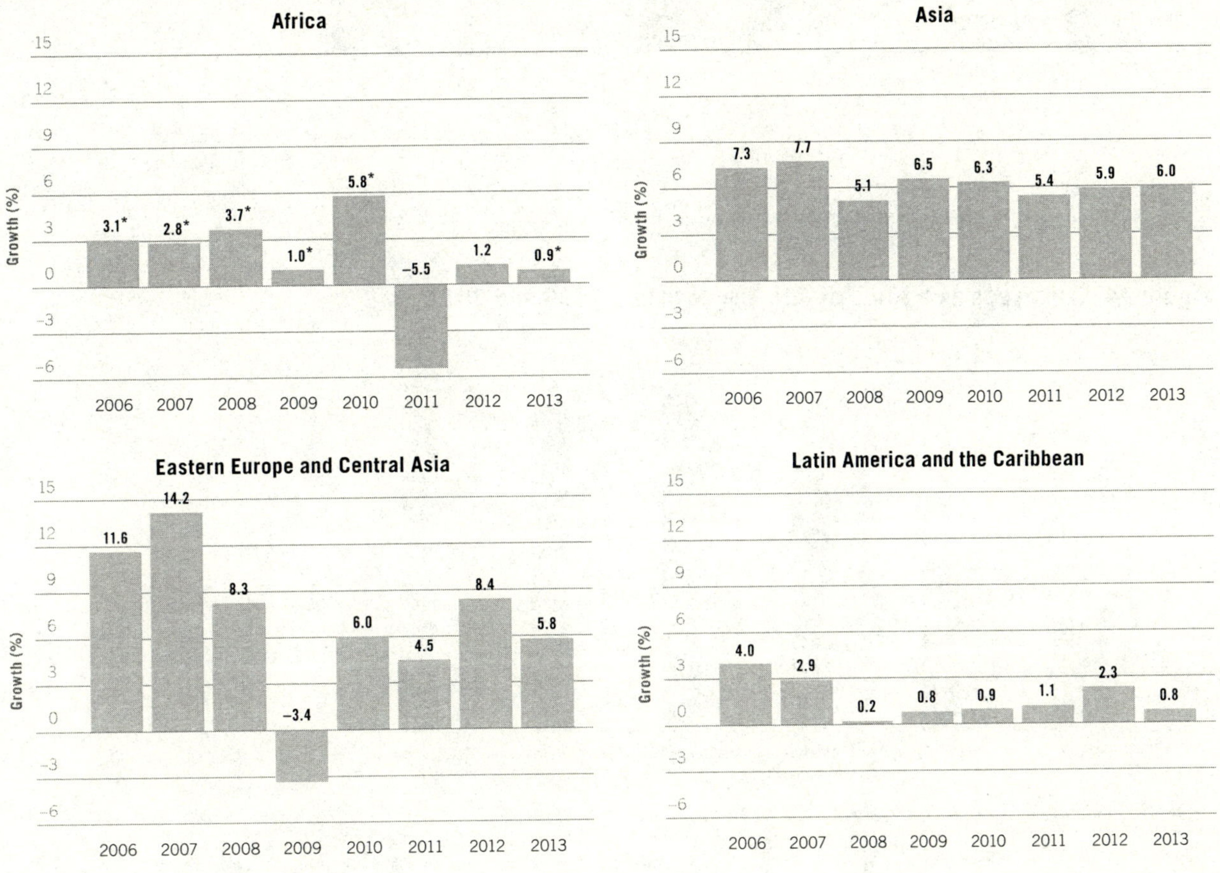

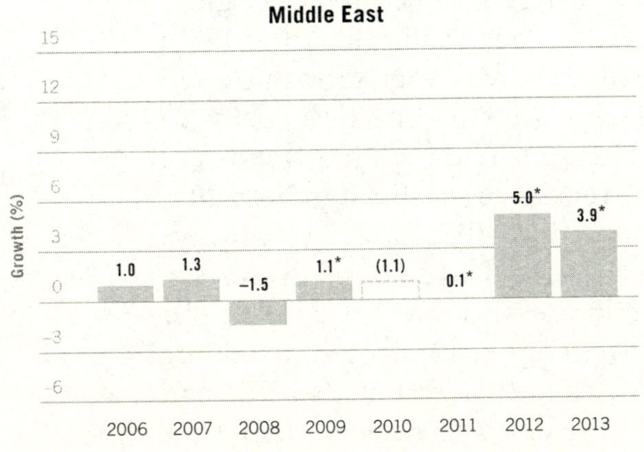

* Growth rates published as "tentative estimates" (based on coverage *c.* 40–74%).

( ) Growth rates published but likely to change (based on coverage of less than 40%).

Note: Regional wage growth is calculated as a weighted average of year-on-year growth in average monthly real wages. For a description of the methodology, see Appendix I.

Source: ILO Global Wage Database. Data accessible at: www.ilo.org/gwr-figures

Figure 13 Real wage growth in the largest emerging and developing economies, 2012–13

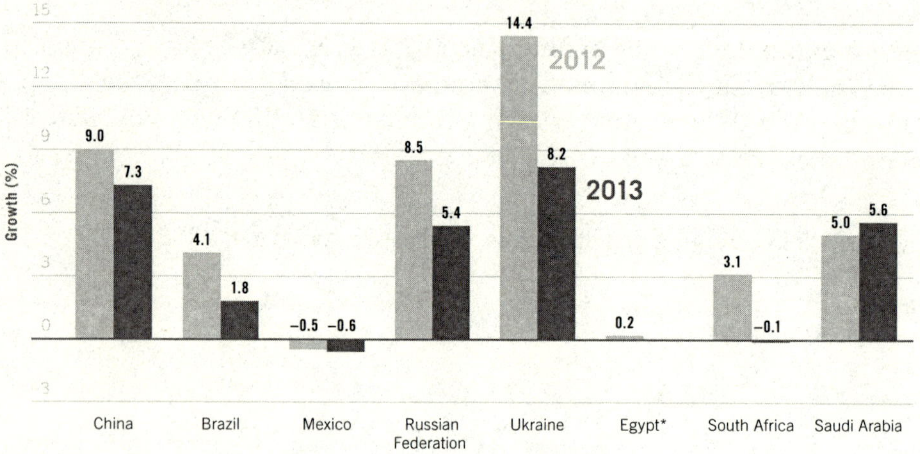

* Data for 2013 are not available for Egypt.

Source: ILO Global Wage Database. Data accessible at: www.ilo.org/gwr-figures

Figure 14 Employees as a share of total employment, 1999 and 2013

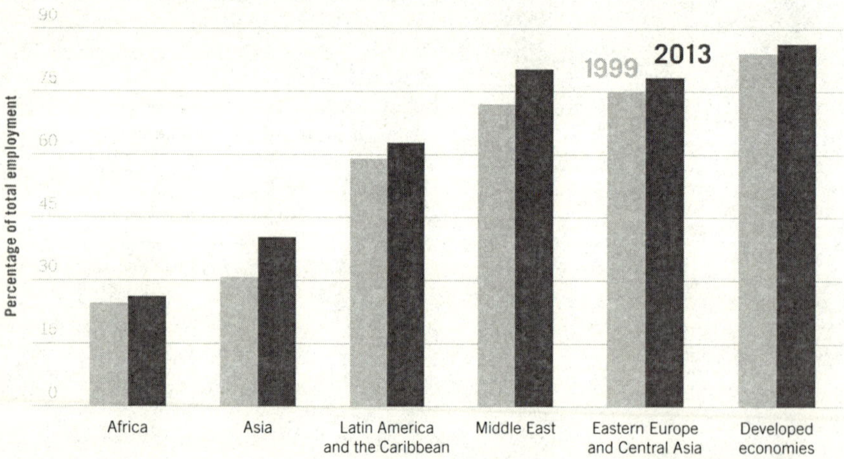

Source: ILO *Trends Econometric Models*, Apr. 2014. Data accessible at: www.ilo.org/gwr-figures

Regional trends are influenced by the largest economies in the region. Figure 13 shows data for the largest countries in the various regions for 2012–13. In Asia, trends are driven largely by China, where average real wage growth slowed in 2013 relative to 2012, but remained high. Real wage growth also slowed between 2012 and 2013 in Latin America and the Caribbean, where regional trends are strongly driven by Brazil and Mexico. In Mexico, real wages declined in both 2012 and 2013, whereas in Brazil real wage growth slowed in 2013. Slowing real wage growth in 2013 in the Russian Federation and Ukraine drove trends in Eastern Europe and Central Asia. In Africa, there are considerable data constraints (for this reason, certain years are marked as tentative in figure 12). Notwithstanding these limitations, real wage growth declined in Africa in 2011, resumed in 2012 and slowed in 2013, in significant measure because of reduced or negative real wage growth in South Africa. Recent trends in the Middle East can be only tentatively formulated, also owing to data constraints, but are driven in large part by Saudi Arabia. As noted in box 2, the specific real wage growth rates for individual countries can be found in the ILO Global Wage Database.

In emerging and developing economies, data constraints make it difficult to compare wage and labour productivity trends.[16] In addition, labour productivity refers to output per worker, while wages refer only to a subcategory of the working population, namely employees. Employees typically represent about 85 per cent of employment in developed countries, but in emerging and developing economies this proportion is often much lower, and changes more rapidly (see figure 14). For this reason, a more appropriate comparison in this group of countries would be between wages and the labour productivity of employees only. Unfortunately, such data are generally not available. All of these issues create some uncertainty in analyses related to wages and productivity in emerging and developing economies. As a result, subsequent analyses for this group of countries focus only on levels and trends in the labour income share, for which data are more widely available.

4.2 Labour income share can decline despite high wage growth

This section highlights levels and trends in the labour income share for a selection of emerging and developing economies. As noted in the previous section, their real wage growth has generally been higher than in developed economies. However, one should not conflate high real wage growth with a growing labour income share; the labour income share can decline despite high real wage growth if labour productivity gains are even higher. In emerging and developing economies, changes in the labour income share often take place in the context of rapid structural change and changing patterns of sectoral employment. Thus, composition effects may be important for explaining changes in the labour income share.

Figure 15 shows the adjusted labour income share for Mexico and Turkey (two of the larger countries among the group of emerging and developing economies and for which data are available from the AMECO database). The decline in the labour income share of Turkey since 1999 has been attributed to a combination of higher capital inflows, financial liberalization and a decline in the labour income share in manufacturing following trade liberalization and increased competition from low-wage economies (Oyvat, 2011). In Mexico, productivity grew faster than wages, and this is reflected in the decline in the labour income share since the early 2000s.

Looking at the unadjusted labour income share, because the adjusted labour income share is not available, the labour income share in China has decreased since the early 2000s (figure 16). Various explanations have been offered for this decline despite the rapid increase in wages. These include structural transformation from the agricultural to non-agricultural sectors, where capital is typically higher, and a decline in the labour income share in industry, attributed by some to the restructuring of state-owned enterprises and expanded monopoly power (Bai and Qian, 2010). Others interpret the declining labour income share as consistent with surplus labour, where productivity gains lead to higher corporate profits and

Figure 15 Adjusted labour income share in Mexico and Turkey, 1995–2013

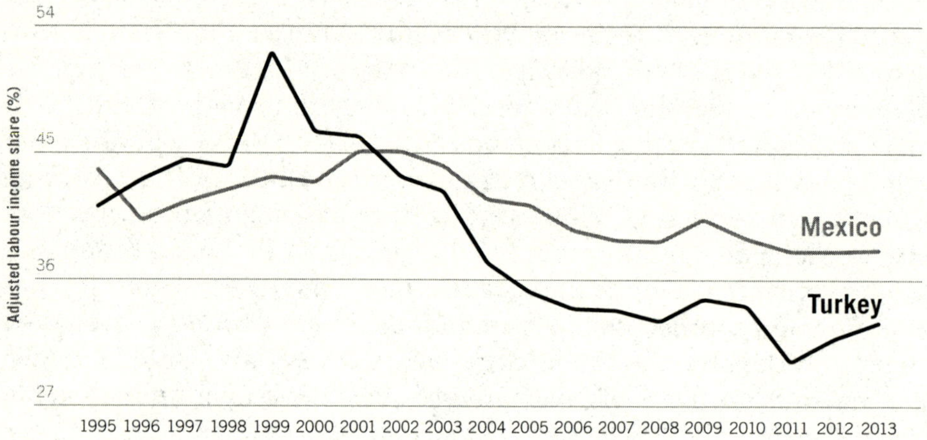

Note: Adjusted wage share, total economy, as a percentage of GDP at current market prices (compensation per employee as a percentage of GDP at market prices per person employed).
Source: European Commission AMECO database. Data accessible at: www.ilo.org/gwr-figures

Figure 16 Unadjusted labour income share in China, 1992–2011

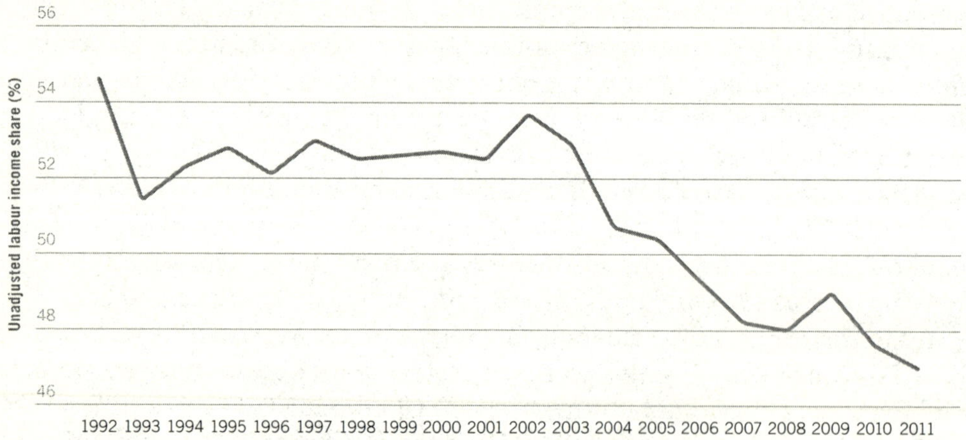

Source: ILO calculations based on data from the *China Statistical Yearbook*, various years.
Data accessible at: www.ilo.org/gwr-figures

more investment, but where wage increases in the industrial sector are limited by the availability of labourers from rural areas (Das and N'Diaye, 2013).

By contrast, in the Russian Federation the labour income share has increased. The available data offer several measures of the labour income share; figure 17 presents two measures from official sources. The first measure ("without hidden compensation") is based on observed wages. The second is adjusted to include an estimate of "hidden wages" and mixed income. Mixed income refers to the income received by the owners of household unincorporated enterprises with and without paid employees (CEC, IMF, OECD, UN and World Bank, 2009, para. 4.160). The second measure is that used to generate the main official estimate of the aggregate labour income share. While these two measures diverge in level, they follow each

Figure 17 Labour income share in the Russian Federation, 1995–2012

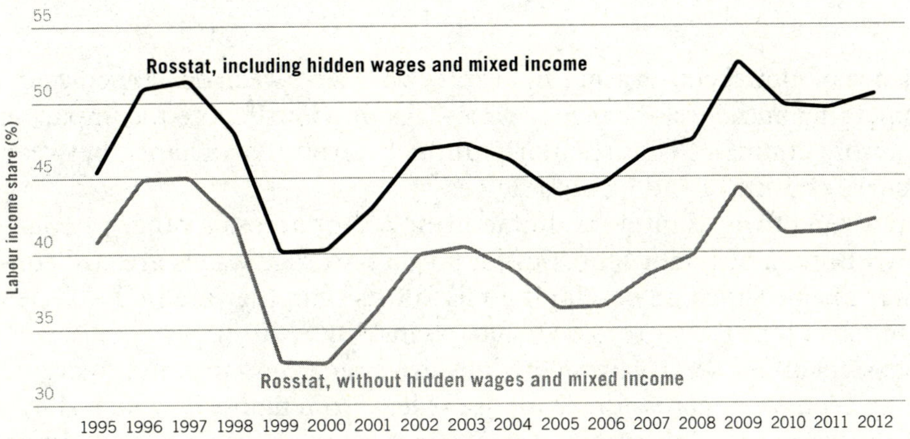

Source: Rosstat (see Lukyanova, forthcoming). Data accessible at: www.ilo.org/gwr-figures

Figure 18 Evolution of labour productivity and wages in South Africa, 1994–2011

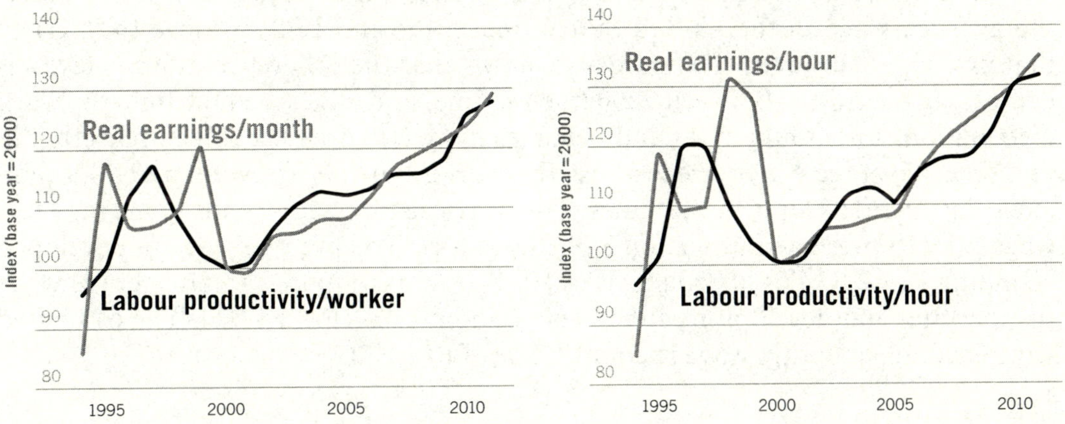

Source: Wittenberg, 2014. Data accessible at: www.ilo.org/gwr-figures

other closely in trajectory. The shift away from traditional sectors (agriculture, transport, manufacturing) towards services between 1995 to 2002 is advanced as one explanation, although within-sector increases in the labour share appear to be the dominant source of the overall growth in the aggregate labour income share (Lukyanova, forthcoming).

In the case of South Africa, where the distribution of productivity gains is a matter of debate, trends in wages and labour productivity using the Post-Apartheid Labour Market Series (PALMS)[17] show that on average – at least since the year 2000 – wages and productivity have largely moved in tandem (figure 18) (Wittenberg, 2014).[18] However, national accounts data show a decline in the unadjusted labour income share for the same period (UNdata, 2014).

5 Towards a progressive convergence in average wages?

Is there evidence of global convergence in average wages between developed economies and emerging and developing economies? As previously noted, comparing wage levels across countries is particularly difficult given the variance between definitions, survey coverage and methodologies.

A comparison of wages in the manufacturing sector across a range of countries by the US Bureau of Labor Statistics found that average wages are still considerably lower in emerging and developing economies than they are in developed economies, but also that the gap is slowly narrowing (BLS, 2012).

The persistent difference in wages between developed economies and emerging and developing economies across the world is evident from figure 19, which shows the shape of the world distribution of average wages if the abovementioned differences between countries' wage data are disregarded and country wages in local currency are converted to purchasing power parity dollars (PPP$), which capture the difference in the cost of living between countries.[19] The difference in wage levels between the emerging and developing economies (on the left side of the distribution) and the developed economies (on the right) is quite substantial. For instance, the average wage in the United States, measured in PPP$, is more than triple that in China. However, the figure also shows that the difference in wage levels is decreasing over time. Between 2000 (the red line) and 2012 (the blue line) the wage distribution shifts to the right and becomes more compressed; this implies that in real terms average wages grew across the world, but they grew by much more in emerging and developing economies. This is consistent with trends in average real wage growth presented in section 3 of this report. The average wage in developed economies in 2013 lies at around US$ (PPP) 3,000 compared to an average wage in emerging and developing economies of about US$ (PPP) 1,000. The estimated world average monthly wage is about US$ (PPP) 1,600.

Figure 19 Global average monthly wage distribution in 2000 and 2012 (2012 PPP$)

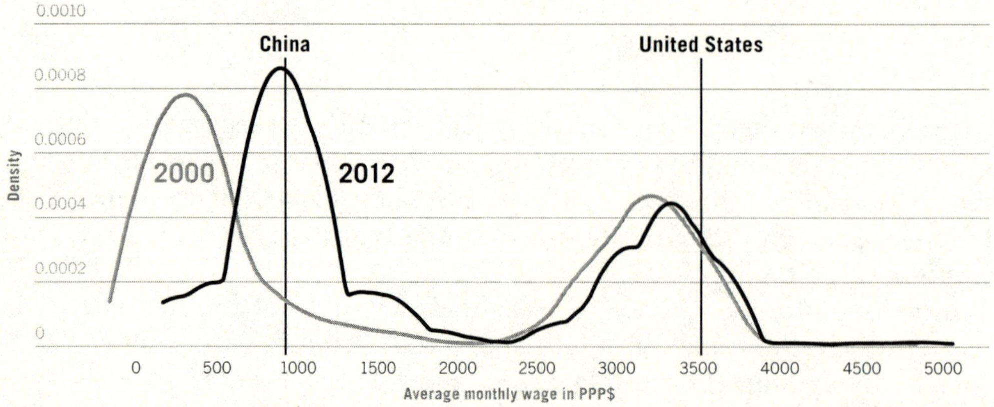

Note: Refers to countries for which wage levels for 2000 and 2012 are available, and covers 83 countries which represent 73 per cent of the world's employees. Wage levels have been converted to constant 2012 PPP$: PPP$1 is equivalent to the purchasing power of US$1 in the United States.

Source: ILO Global Wage Database. Data accessible at: www.ilo.org/gwr-figures

PART II Wages and income inequality

6 Introduction: The role of wages in household income inequality

6.1 The context: Long-term inequality on the rise in many countries since the 1980s

Part I of the report looked at one dimension of distribution: the distribution of national income between labour and capital. Part II of the report examines how the distribution of wages contributes to household inequality within countries.

Growing inequality has gained much attention in recent years.[20] A large and expanding literature has shown that inequality, measured in various ways, has been increasing in a majority of developed economies in recent decades. The OECD, for example, has documented in detail the rise in inequality in about two-thirds of developed economies between the early 1980s and the financial crisis of 2008–09 (see OECD, 2008; OECD, 2011). In some countries, including the United States and the United Kingdom, the rise in inequality has been particularly stark (Salverda, Nolan and Smeeding, 2009b, p. 5), although top income shares have increased in other countries too (Piketty, 2013).

Emerging and developing economies – where household income inequality is often greater than in developed economies – have also not been immune from this trend: between the 1990s and the 2000s inequality increased in a majority of such countries for which household survey data are readily available (Ferreira and Ravallion, 2009; see also Goldberg and Pavcnik, 2007). However, the trend is not universal. In several Latin American countries, wage and household income distributions have narrowed, often from a high level, between the mid-1990s and the onset of the global economic crisis (Gasparini, Cruces and Tornarolli, 2009).

There appears to be a growing consensus that high levels of inequality can be problematic for several reasons. While some level of inequality is a natural outcome of heterogeneity in personal characteristics, providing incentives for people to invest in education and make efforts at work, high and rising income inequality can become an obstacle to "equality of opportunity" and lead to less social mobility. With high inequality, economic advantage is more likely to be inherited than earned (Corak, 2013).[21] This can discourage individual effort as well as damage perceptions of fairness in society and also adversely affect social outcomes and social cohesion (d'Hombres, Weber and Elia, 2012; Jencks, 2002).

Inequality has also been shown to undermine economic growth. Recent work by the IMF shows that more inequality reduces "the pace and durability of growth" (Ostry, Berg and Tsangarides, 2014), while OECD research shows that greater social and economic inclusion is strongly associated with longer and stronger periods of sustained economic growth (OECD, 2014a). Although the links between inequality and growth are complex,[22] increasing attention has been devoted to the adverse effects of inequality on health and education, on political and economic stability, and on the social consensus required for well-functioning societies. Inequality has also been highlighted as a factor increasing risk of crisis, and as one of the possible causes of the 2008 financial crisis in the United States (see for example Rajan, 2010; Palley and Horn, 2013; Sturn and Van Treeck, 2013; Kumhof and Rancière, 2010; Krueger, 2012). By redistributing income from poorer to richer households, growing inequality may have exerted downward pressure on aggregate demand (as richer households have a lower propensity to consume their income than poorer households) and encouraged many families to borrow beyond their means to try to maintain their consumption levels.

6.2 The range of policy responses to inequality

Much of the debate on potential policy responses to growing inequality focuses on redistribution through fiscal policies (OECD, 2014a; IMF, 2014b). The IMF considers fiscal policy (which includes both taxes and transfers) as "the primary tool for governments to affect income distribution", and suggests that "both tax and expenditure policies need to be carefully designed to balance distributional and efficiency objectives" (IMF, 2014b, p. 1). It has been estimated that in developed economies, fiscal policies reduce income inequality, by an average of about one-quarter (OECD, 2011) to one-third (IMF, 2014b). The ILO has highlighted in particular the role of social protection systems in reducing inequality and contributing to more inclusive growth (ILO, 2014f).[23] Progressive personal income taxes and in-work benefits (such as tax credits to low-income workers) play an important role, but in practice most of the reduction is achieved on the expenditure side through transfers. In emerging and developing economies, where tax revenues and social transfers are lower, and indirect taxes dominate, fiscal policies play a much smaller role in redistribution (IMF, 2014b). In both contexts, there is definitely scope for reform to achieve more redistribution.[24]

However, a focus on the role of the labour market is important, too. The OECD (2011) documented how in developed economies, in the decades before the crisis, greater wage inequality had been the single most important driver of income inequality.

Part II of this report extends the existing analysis of the relationship between the distribution of wages and the distribution of household income. Section 7 looks at recent trends in household income inequality in developed economies in the crisis years, and also at trends in emerging and developing economies over roughly the last decade. Section 8 then studies the role of wages in explaining these recent trends. In particular, the report decomposes changes in income inequality with a view to better understanding the role of wages, employment and other factors in these changes. Seeking to better comprehend how wages can affect household income inequality, section 9 of the report breaks down the income sources of households located at different places in the distribution of income, in different countries. Information on the income sources of different groups of households can shed light on how different available policy instruments may be appropriate to reduce inequality. Finally, in section 10, the report decomposes wage gaps for women, migrants and workers in the informal economy between an "explained" component and an "unexplained" penalty (which refers to factors that are "not accounted for" by those observed human capital and labour market characteristics that should in principle explain wage differences).

At the broadest level, increasing inequality in the labour market will place a heavier burden on reducing inequality through secondary (tax and transfer) redistribution mechanisms. These mechanisms have been declining in their impact as inequality grows, and further redistribution may face political and other constraints, notably when directed to the working age population. Therefore, many governments may wish to consider addressing the problem of rising inequality also through policy measures that directly address distribution in the labour market. Part III of this report thus turns to policy response and examines the range of policies available.

7 Mixed recent trends in income inequality

7.1 Measuring "top–bottom" and "middle-class" inequality

This section documents recent trends in the distribution of total per capita household income inequality (hereinafter termed *income inequality* or simply *inequality*), where total household income is defined following the Canberra Group as including income from employment, property and transfers, before the payment of taxes and other transfers paid (for definitions, see Appendix II).[25] A sample of developed and emerging and developing economies is covered. No single inequality measure is perfect, but two measures of inequality are used to assess: (1) the distance between the top and the bottom 10 per cent within countries (also referred to as deciles); and (2) the extent to which inequality has changed among the middle class, within countries.[26] Only households in which at least one member is of working age are considered in the analysis, and income is adjusted for household size (see Appendix II).

A purely statistical definition of the term "middle class" is used with a view to identifying whether the statistical middle group of the distribution has become more "stretched" and dissimilar or, on the contrary, more "compressed" and similar (for a more sociological discussion of the middle class, see box 5). Since long-term trends already under way before the crisis are well documented,[27] this report covers trends over the crisis period, with a first data point before the crisis and a last point with the latest available data. For the most part, the analysis covers the period from 2006 to 2010 in developed economies, and a slightly longer period in emerging and developing economies. The estimates provide information on the extent to which earlier trends have continued during the crisis, and give some clues as to how the cost of the crisis has been distributed across different social groups.

"Top–bottom" inequality is measured by comparing the top and the bottom of the income distribution: see figure 20, where each person represents 10 per

Box 5 What is understood by the term "middle class"?

In developed economies, many people define themselves as middle class, and so the idea represents a shared sense of how most people in a society live. In emerging and developing economies, being middle class is typically more of an aspiration, representing how most people would *like* to live.

Economists sometimes represent the middle class as an *average class* located in an interval of 75 per cent to 125 per cent of the median income (Thurow, 1987, cited by Ravallion, 2010). But most authors agree that great heterogeneity characterizes the middle class. Consequently, notions such as *lower middle class, upper middle class* and even *old vs new middle class* (Chauvel, 2006) have appeared, conveying a certain difficulty in providing an accurate and precise definition. When it comes to emerging and developing economies, authors are confronted with the difficulty of applying a notion that is linked to the Western context. Ravallion simply considers that "someone is middle class if that person would not be considered poor in any developing country, implying a lower bound of $9 a day" (Ravallion, 2010, p. 452).

From an economic point of view, the middle class is considered the driver of modern consumption societies (Kharas, 2010). From a sociological perspective, the formation of a social class includes other factors: a specific economic position (possibly creating conflicts of interest with other social classes) and a consciousness of having similar conditions (Chauvel, 2006, p. 31). Today in Western societies, relatively high levels of consumption of goods and services define, or are a major attribute of, the middle class. Some identify this increasing consumption as consumerism and argue that this profoundly changes traditional social relations within the middle class because people tend to be more individualistic than class-oriented (Trentmann, 2004), and social relations are driven by more hedonistic and individualistic patterns (Migone, 2007). In this view, both factors contribute to the erosion of the class identity in all societies.

In emerging and developing economies, such consumption is still perceived more as a privilege of the *upper* middle class than as a unifying social force, as in Western-based societies.[1]

[1] The example of Viet Nam is quite interesting: see Dormeier Freire, 2009.

Source: Alexandre Dormeier Freire, Graduate Institute of International and Development Studies, Geneva (2014).

cent of the population. The measure of "top–bottom inequality" (also termed the D9/D1 ratio) is the ratio between two cut-off points: the threshold value above which individuals are in the top 10 per cent and the threshold value below which they are in the bottom 10 per cent of the distribution. Figure 20 also sets out the boundaries of what is understood in this report as constituting "lower", "middle" and "upper" income groups. Middle-class inequality (D7/D3) is measured by cutting out the top and the bottom 30 per cent of the distribution and comparing the "entry point" and the "exit point" of a statistical middle, comprising the 40 per cent of individuals grouped around the median (as shown in figure 20).

Figure 20 Measures of inequality

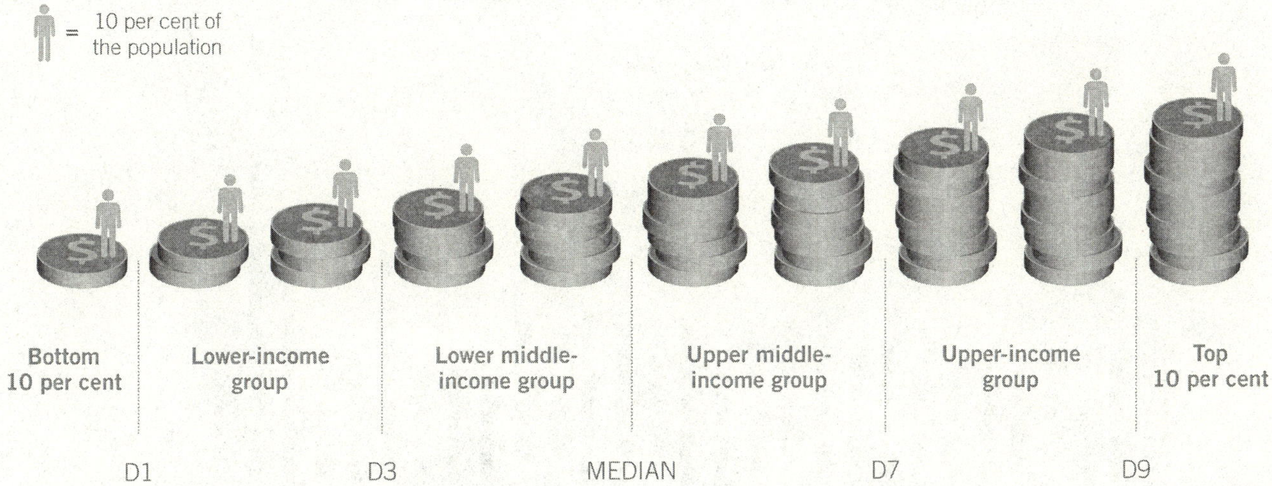

7.2 Developed economies: Mixed inequality trends in a context of generally flat or declining incomes

In our sample of developed economies, between 2006 and 2010 "top–bottom inequality" increased in about half of the countries, and decreased or remained stable in the remaining countries. Figure 21(a) shows these trends with countries ordered from left to right, from the countries where inequality decreased to those where it increased. Using the methodology and data sources described in Appendix II, inequality increased most in Spain and the United States (where inequality, measured by the D9/D1 ratio, is highest), and declined most in Bulgaria and Romania.

Over the same period, trends in middle-class inequality in developed economies have also been mixed, increasing in about half the countries where a change can be observed and decreasing in the other half (figure 21(b)). Countries are again ordered from left to right, starting with the countries where inequality decreased most and moving to the countries where it increased most. We see that according to our methodology, the country where inequality among the middle class increased most is Ireland, followed by Spain. On the other side, Romania and the Netherlands are the two countries in the sample where inequality among the middle class fell most. The United Kingdom is one example of a country where middle-class inequality increased while top–bottom inequality remained more or less stable and even declined somewhat.

The "flattening effect" of the crisis on incomes

In developed economies, these mixed trends frequently took place in a context of stagnating or declining household incomes between 2007 and 2009/10 (see figure 23). With the exception of Spain, where inequality increased, some of the countries most adversely affected by the crisis have seen a reduction in inequality as a result of a general downward "flattening effect" of the crisis, meaning that incomes have fallen more for high-income than for lower-income households. Thus, inequality

Figure 21 Inequality in a sample of developed economies in the crisis years, 2006–10: (a) top–bottom inequality (D9/D1); (b) middle-class inequality (D7/D3)

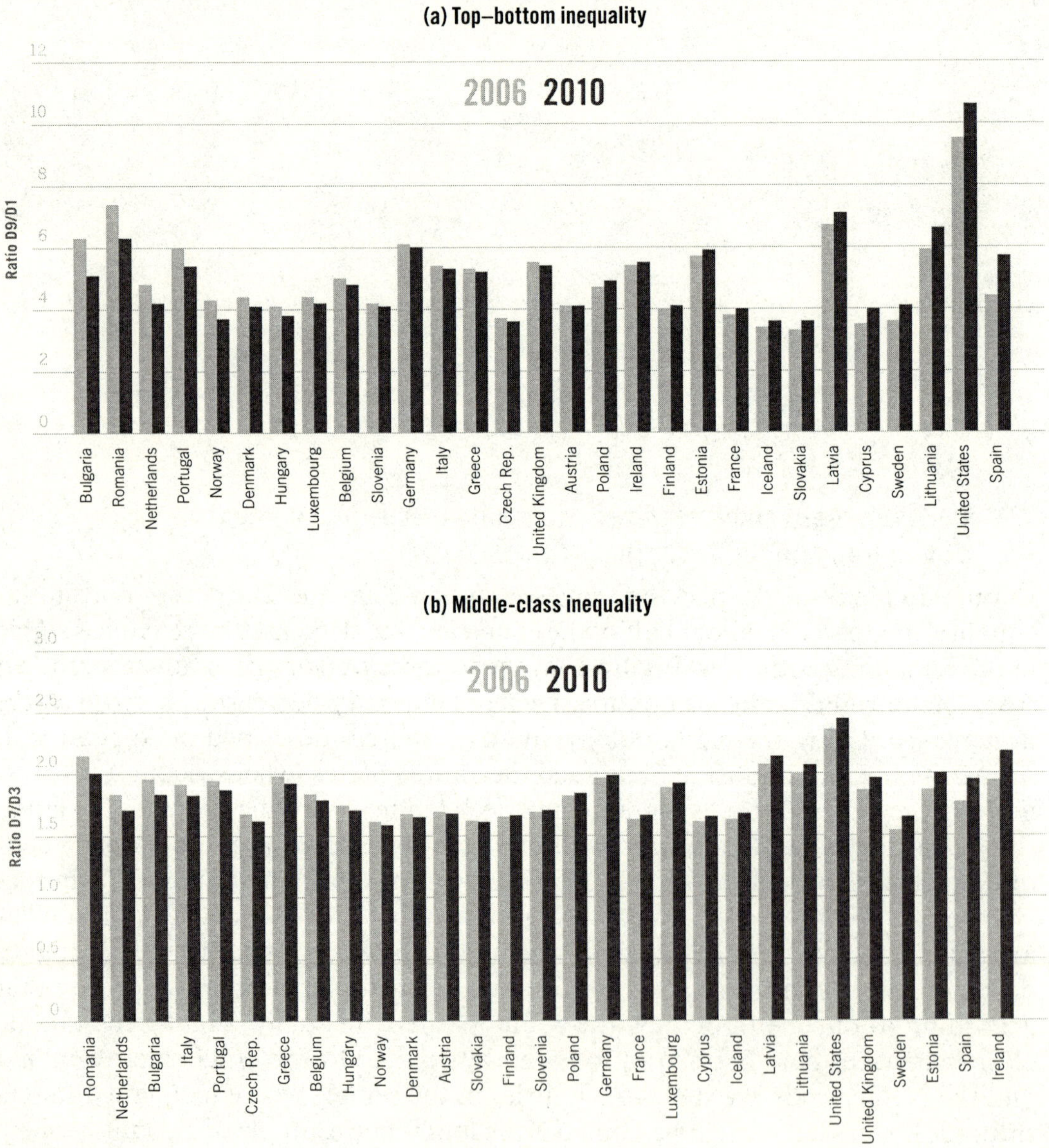

Note: For methodology, definitions and database, see Appendix II.

Source: ILO estimates. Data accessible at: www.ilo.org/gwr-figures

declined in Romania and Portugal and remained almost unchanged in Greece, three countries severely hit by the crisis.[28] A few countries, such as Denmark, the Netherlands and Norway, have been able to combine growing household income and falling inequality during this period.

7.3 Emerging and developing economies: Varying inequality in a context of generally increasing incomes

In our sample of emerging and developing economies, "top–bottom inequality" has decreased over the last decade in about half of all countries, and has remained stable or increased in the other half (figure 22(a)). Measuring inequality in emerging and developing economies is sometimes difficult due to data limitations, and levels of inequality may not be strictly comparable across countries (for more discussion on the data, see Appendix II). A longer time frame is considered here since the crisis did not affect most of these countries as much as it did the developed economies. The longer time frame also captures some of the structural changes countries may have undergone during the period. Our estimates suggest that top–bottom inequality fell most in Brazil and Argentina, and also declined in China,[29]

Figure 22 Inequality in a sample of emerging and developing economies over the past decade: (a) top–bottom inequality (D9/D1); (b) middle-class inequality (D7/D3)

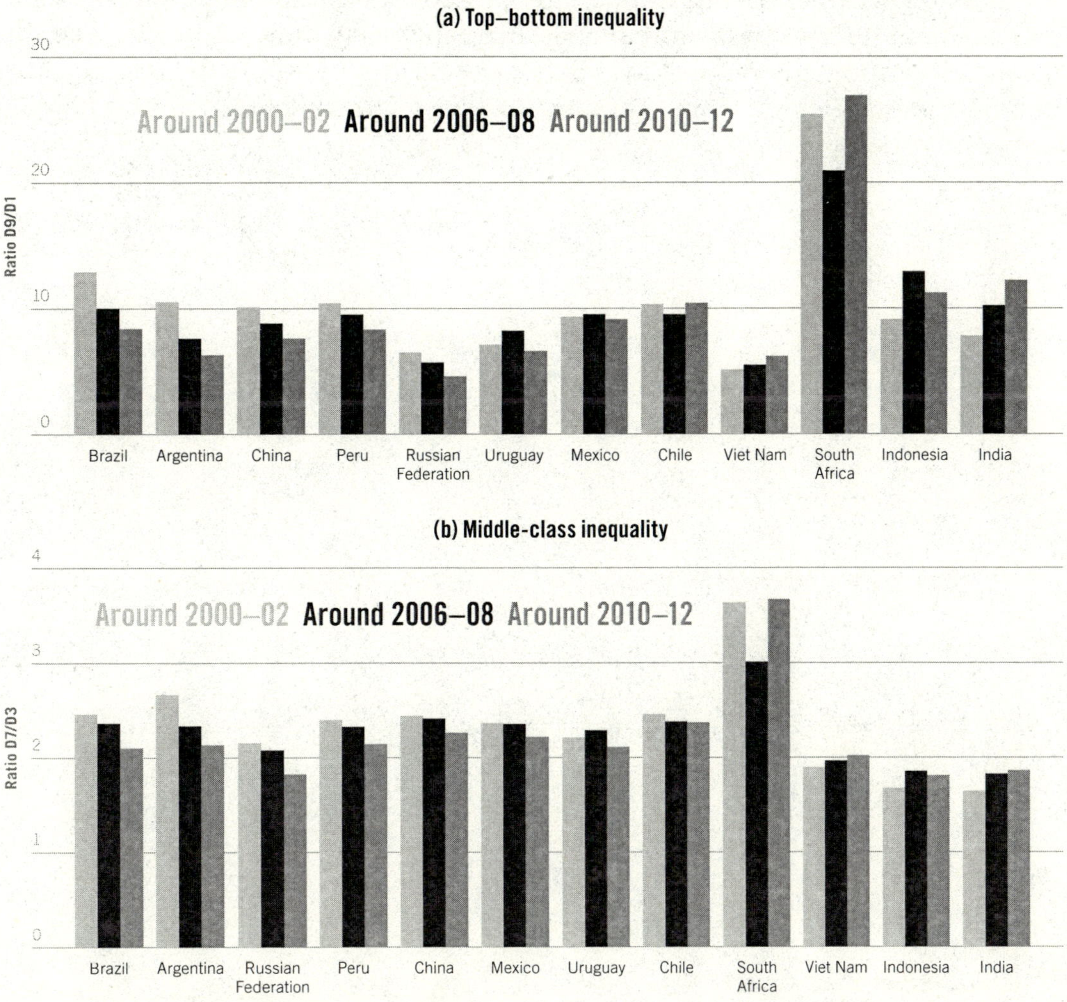

Note: For methodology, definitions and database, see Appendix II.

Source: ILO estimates. Data accessible at: www.ilo.org/gwr-figures

Peru, the Russian Federation and Uruguay.[30] Among the countries in our sample, inequality increased most in India and Indonesia. It also increased in Viet Nam, from a relatively low level, and in South Africa, from a very high level inherited from the apartheid era. In South Africa, the rise in inequality during 2007–11 occurred because the income growth of bottom decile households stagnated in real terms, while that of top decile households continued to increase at about the same rate as in the earlier period.

Turning to the middle class, we see that inequality decreased in almost two-thirds of our sample of emerging and developing economies, and remained stable or increased in the remaining countries (figure 22(b)). In Argentina, Brazil and the Russian Federation, middle-class inequality declined substantially. By contrast, it remained unchanged in South Africa and increased in India, Indonesia and Viet Nam.

In contrast to developed economies, in emerging and developing economies these trends frequently took place in a context of increasing household incomes (see figure 23). A comparison of figures 21 and 22 also shows that total inequality remains higher in emerging and developing economies than in developed economies even after progress on reducing inequality in the former group. The difference is particularly marked in top–bottom inequality, while the middle class, though more stretched, shows a proportionally smaller difference in inequality.

Figure 23 Recent evolution of real household income in selected countries

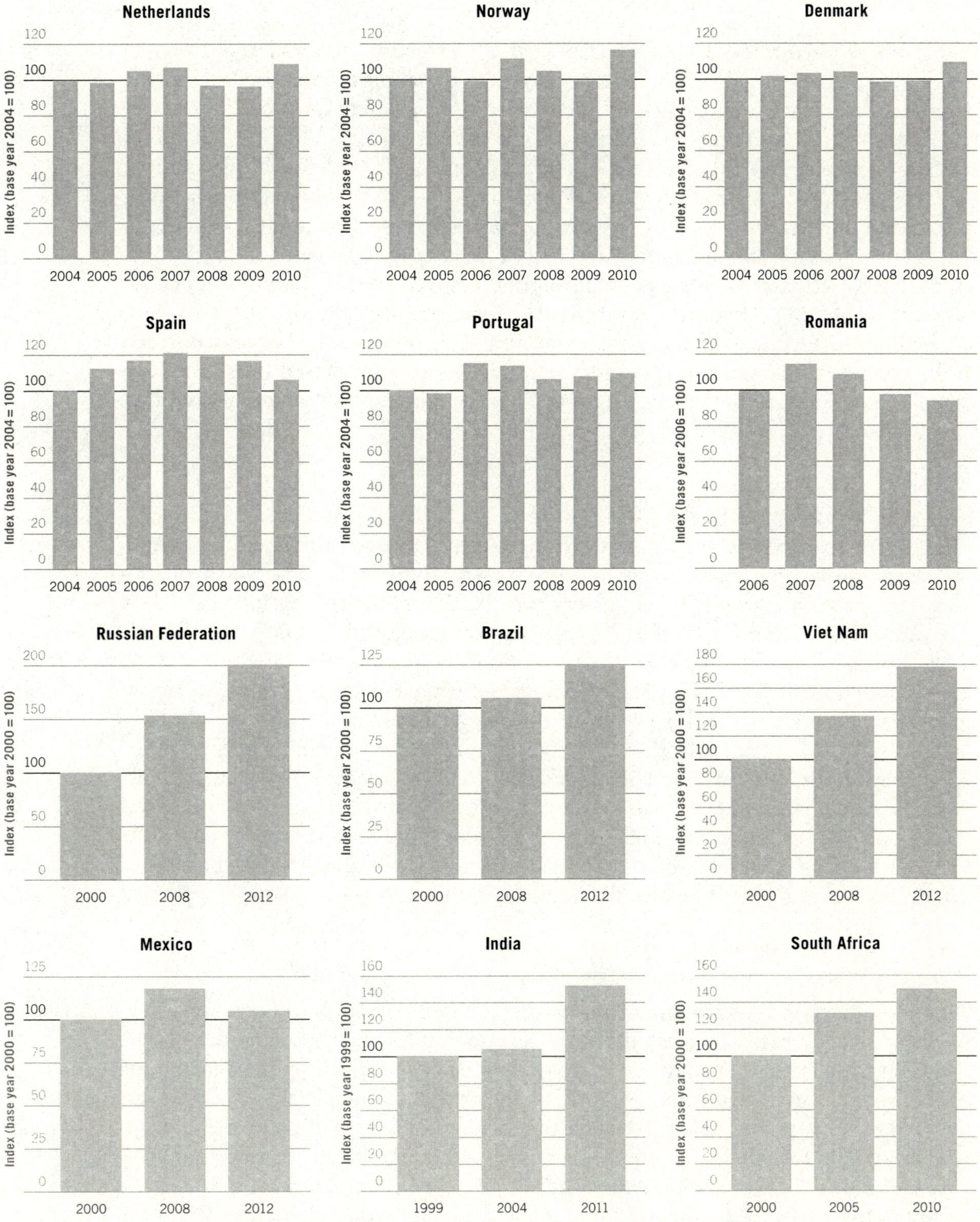

Note: For methodology, definitions and databases, see Appendix II.

Source: ILO estimates. Data accessible at: www.ilo.org/gwr-figures

8 Inequality: The role of wages and paid employment

What has been the role of wages in recent inequality trends? Total household income inequality can change for many reasons. Household income is composed of income from employment, property income, income from the production of household services for own use, and transfers received.[31] The overall change in income inequality is therefore the sum of the changes of these components (for a detailed explanation, see Appendix III). For the purposes of both analysis and policy-making, it is important to understand which of these components drives or dominates changes in inequality. To what extent can recent trends in inequality be explained by changes in the distribution of wages as compared to changes in the distribution of other sources of income? Given the multiplicity of factors that can in theory explain inequality, identifying the main forces at play is of importance for an informed policy debate on how in some countries trends towards increased inequality can be reversed, and on what lessons to draw from the reduction in inequality in other countries.

8.1 Analysing how wages affect changes in inequality

The extent to which recent changes in inequality have been driven by changes in wages, rather than by changes in other income sources, is explored through a decomposition methodology. In general terms, the methodology introduced by DiNardo, Fortin and Lemieux (1996) and further employed by Daly and Valletta (2004) proceeds as follows: (1) decompose household income by income source; (2) observe how the level of inequality changed during a given period; and (3) compare the actual change in inequality to the change in inequality that would have been observed if the distribution of wages had remained unchanged during the same period (the "counterfactual"). The difference between the "counterfactual" level of inequality and the actual level of inequality provides an estimate of the effect of wages on the change in inequality.[32] The same method (described more fully in Appendix III) can be used to identify and estimate the contribution of other income sources to the observed change in inequality.

8.2 The labour market effect: Wage effect plus employment effect

At the household level, income from wages depends on both the level of wages received by members who are paid employees and on the number of members who are paid employees. Indeed, when undertaking the decomposition, the distribution of household wages is affected not only by the change in the distribution of wages of paid employees, but also by the fact that wages fall to zero if some members of the household lose their jobs as paid employees, or increase from zero to a positive value when a household member gets a job as paid employee. If a household member loses his or her job and is eligible for unemployment benefits, wages fall to zero and unemployment benefits turn positive. As illustrated in figure 24, the labour market effect is therefore the sum of changes in the wages of those who are

Figure 24 The labour market effect: Wage effect and employment effect

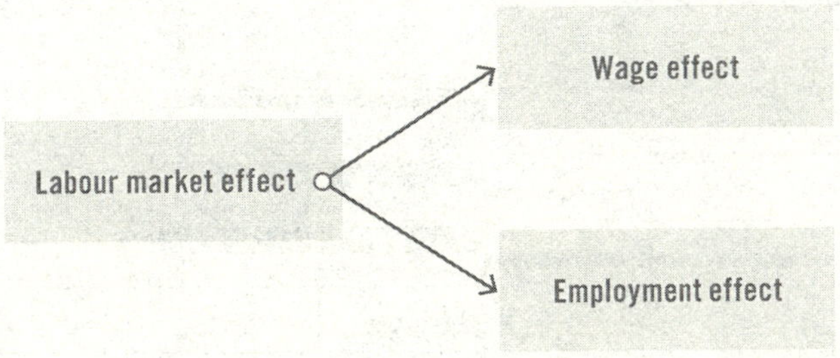

in paid employment at the beginning and end of the period (the "wage effect") and the change in the number of people who are paid employees (the "employment effect"). In our analysis, we separate these two effects.

8.3 Developed economies: Job losses and wage cuts as the major factors in changes in inequality

In developed countries, the labour market effect (i.e. wage plus employment effects) would have increased inequality in two-thirds of countries if other income sources had not offset the increase. In those countries where inequality *did* increase, other income sources offset about one-third of the increase in inequality generated by the labour market effect. Country-specific developments can be seen in figure 25, which shows the findings from the decomposition of "top–bottom inequality" (D9/D1) for developed economies. Countries are ranked from top to bottom, starting with the country where inequality increased most, to the country where it declined most, over the period 2006–10. The ranking of countries is thus the same as in section 7, but figure 25 focuses on the change in (rather than the levels of) top–bottom inequality. In addition to showing the actual change in inequality, the figure shows how much of the change was due, respectively, to the wage effect, to the employment effect and to changes in other sources of income in the household.[33]

Job losses and top–bottom inequality

When looking at countries where top–bottom inequality increased, labour market effects (wage plus employment effects) were more important than other income effects in explaining this increase in a majority of cases. In Spain and the United States, the two countries where inequality increased most, the labour market effect accounted for, respectively, 90 per cent and 140 per cent of the increase in inequality – meaning that in Spain inequality was further increased by other income sources, while in the United States (as in some other countries) other income sources partially offset the increase in inequality caused by the labour market effect. The employment effects dominate the wage effects in countries where inequality increased the most, suggesting that job losses were the major cause of top–bottom inequality in these countries during the crisis. (The bars in figure 25 show that within the labour market effect, the wage effect contributed to

Figure 25 Change in inequality between the top and bottom 10 per cent (D9/D1) in developed economies, 2006–10

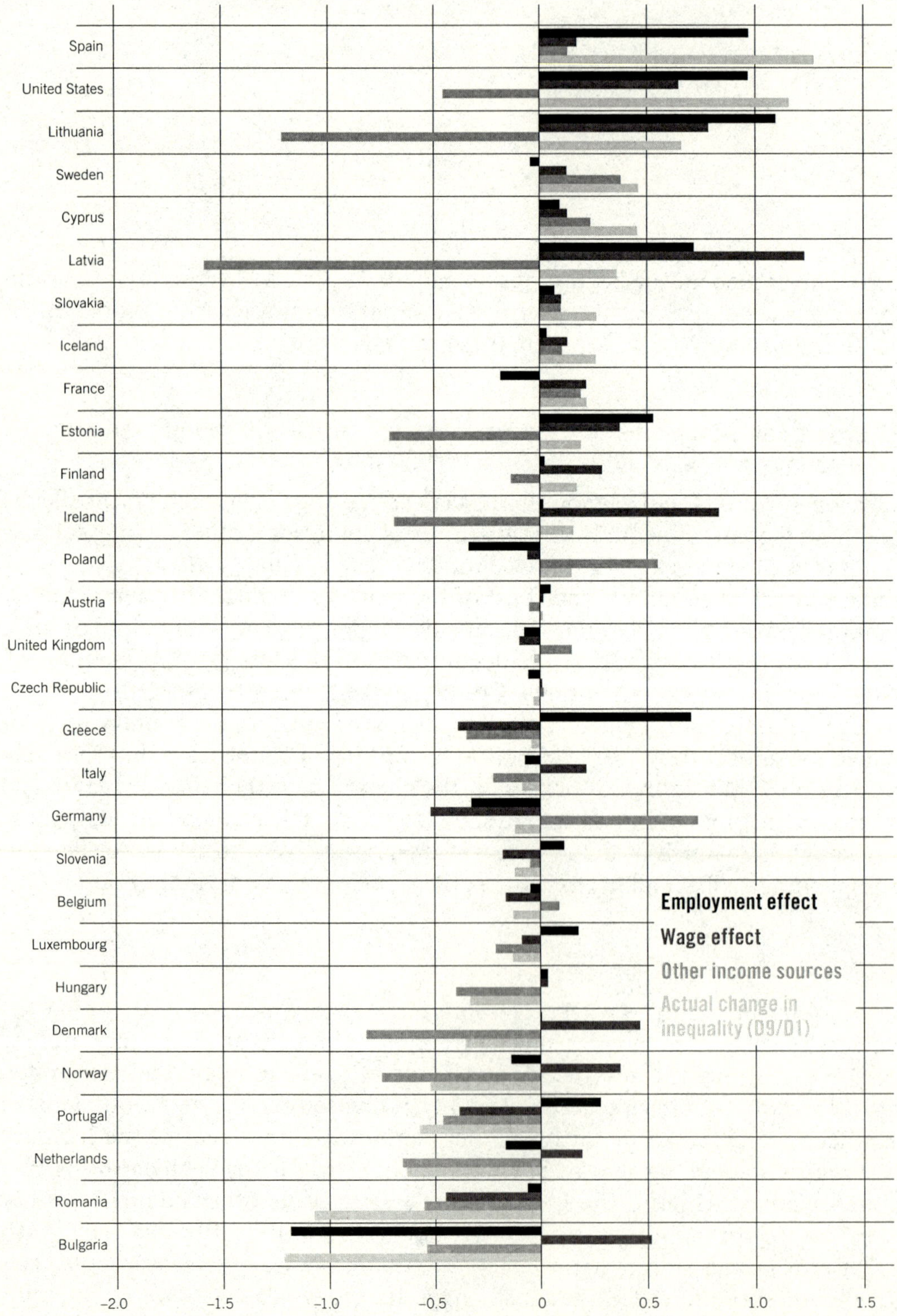

Note: For methodology, definitions and databases, see Appendix II.
Source: ILO estimates. Data accessible at: www.ilo.org/gwr-figures

the overall increase in inequality in both Spain and the United States, but in these two countries the employment effect was even larger, as many workers lost their jobs and hence their wages.)

Among countries where top–bottom inequality declined, this was predominantly a result of the labour market effect in Germany and Belgium. Note that in Greece, Romania and Portugal, the wage effect contributed to less inequality; this occurred because the whole wage distribution was flattened (i.e. wages have fallen more for high-income than for lower-income households). In Bulgaria, Denmark, the Netherlands and Norway, while the wage effect contributed to more inequality, it was more than offset by other factors and inequality declined.

Wages matter more for the middle class

Looking at middle-class inequality (figure 26), the labour market effect contributed to higher inequality in almost three-quarters of the countries in the sample. In countries where inequality increased, other income sources offset only about 5 per cent of the increase. Here again, countries are ranked from top to bottom, from the country where household income inequality increased most, to the country where it declined most, over the period 2006–10. As in the D9/D1 analysis (shown in figure 25), here too the labour market effect is the dominating factor behind the increase in inequality. It is notable, though, that other incomes offset the increase in inequality much less among the middle class (as might be expected, since wages are the major source of household income for the middle classes, as will be seen later in this report).

When looking at middle-class inequality, labour market effect is dominated by changes in the distribution of wages rather than by changes in employment in most countries with increases in middle-class inequality, with Spain the most notable exception. This was the case for example in Ireland, where middle-class inequality increased most, but also in other countries where inequality increased, such as Estonia, Iceland, Sweden and the United States. Considering the labour market effect in those countries where inequality decreased, the decline in inequality was exclusively due to the wage effect in Greece, Portugal and Romania. In Bulgaria and the Netherlands, middle-class inequality fell even though the wage effect pushed towards more inequality.

Taken together, the evidence shows that the labour market effect was the largest force pushing towards more inequality over the period 2006–10; other income sources offset some of these increases in some countries. In this sense, the last few years have been no different from the three decades before the crisis, when other evidence shows that increases in inequality were largely driven by changes in the distribution of wages (see OECD, 2011; Salverda, Nolan and Smeeding, 2009b, p. 11; Daly and Valletta, 2004). The difference is that during the crisis, employment played a larger role in explaining changes in inequality.

Figure 26 Change in inequality within the middle class (D7/D3) in developed economies, 2006–10

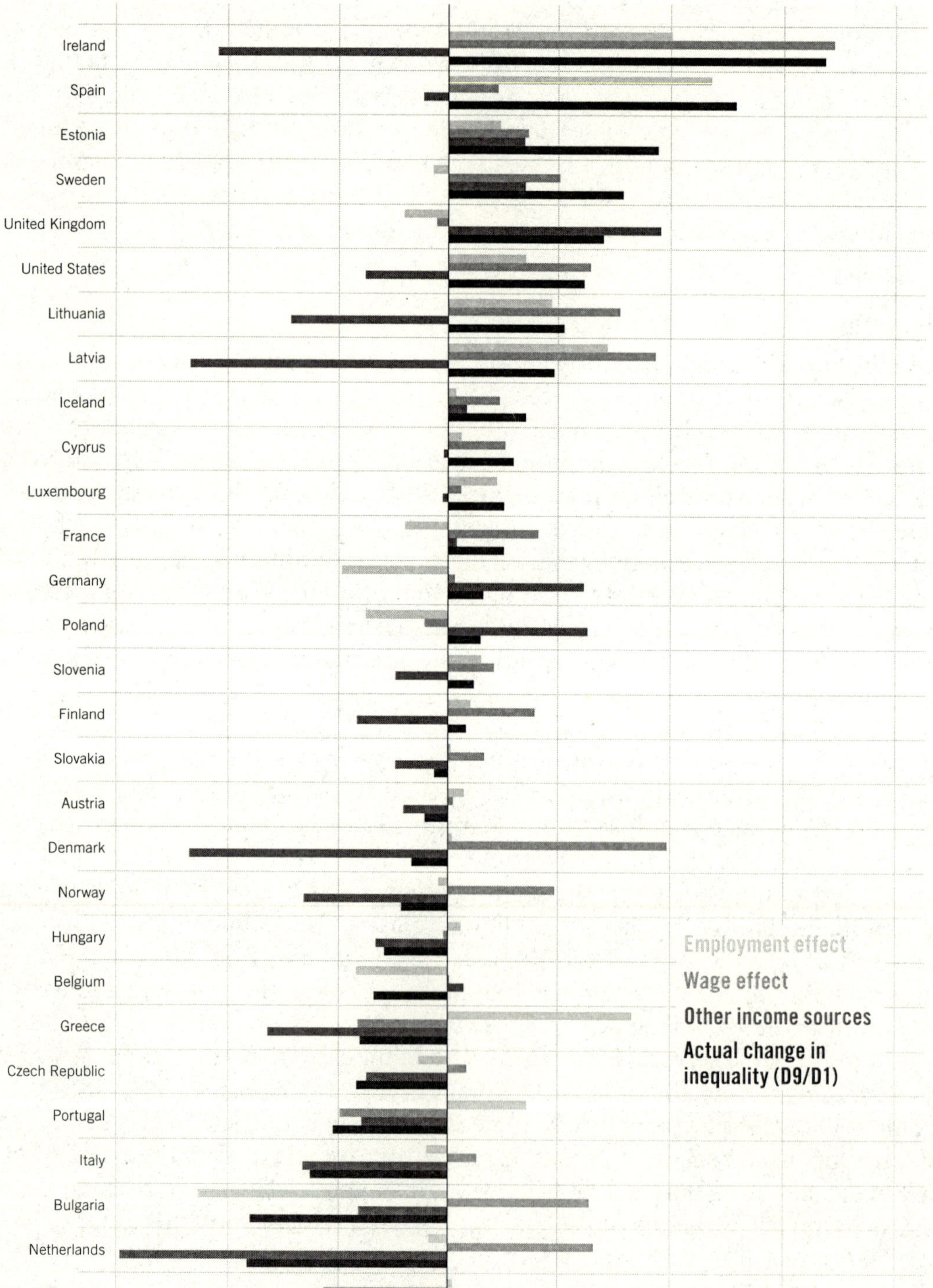

Note: For methodology, definitions and databases, see Appendix II.
Source: ILO estimates. Data accessible at: www.ilo.org/gwr-figures

8.4 Emerging and developing economies: A major role for labour market effects

Among our sample of emerging and developing economies, the labour market has also been an important factor in explaining inequality trends (even though wages account for a smaller proportion of total income in those countries, as will be seen in the next section of the report). In fact, no country in our sample succeeded in reducing top–bottom inequality over the past decade without also reducing inequality in the labour market. However, some countries saw declines in wage inequality while experiencing growing income inequality due to changes in other sources of household income.[34]

Top–bottom inequality: the importance of the labour market

Figure 27 shows the findings from the decomposition of top–bottom inequality (D9/D1) for emerging and developing economies for which data allow the decomposition technique to be applied, covering roughly the last decade. Countries are ranked from top to bottom, from the country where inequality increased most to the one where it declined most. Argentina and Brazil foot the list as the countries where total inequality fell most: the labour market effect accounted for 72 per cent of the decade-long reduction in top–bottom inequality in Brazil and 87 per cent in Argentina. In both countries, other income sources (including transfers) also contributed to the reduction in inequality, and both the wage and employment effects contributed to the reduction in inequality attributable to the labour market. In Peru, the Russian Federation and Uruguay, where inequality also declined, the decline would have been even greater if other income sources had not contributed towards more inequality. In Viet Nam, the decrease due to the wage effect was

Figure 27 Change in inequality between the top and bottom 10 per cent (D9/D1) in selected emerging and developing economies, selected years

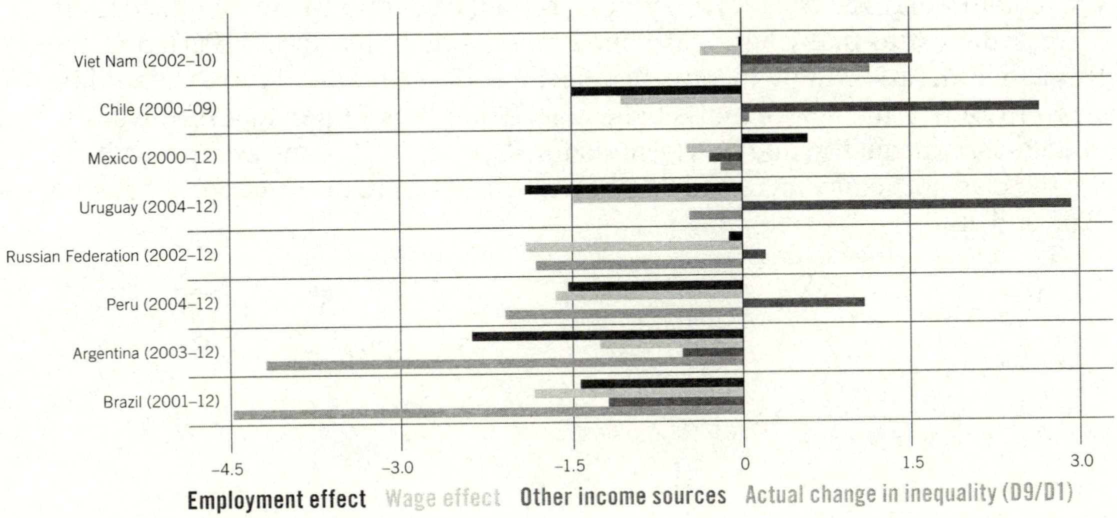

Note: For methodology, definitions and database, see Appendix II.

Source: ILO estimates. Data accessible at: www.ilo.org/gwr-figures

Figure 28 Change in inequality within the middle class (D7/D3) in selected emerging and developing economies, selected years

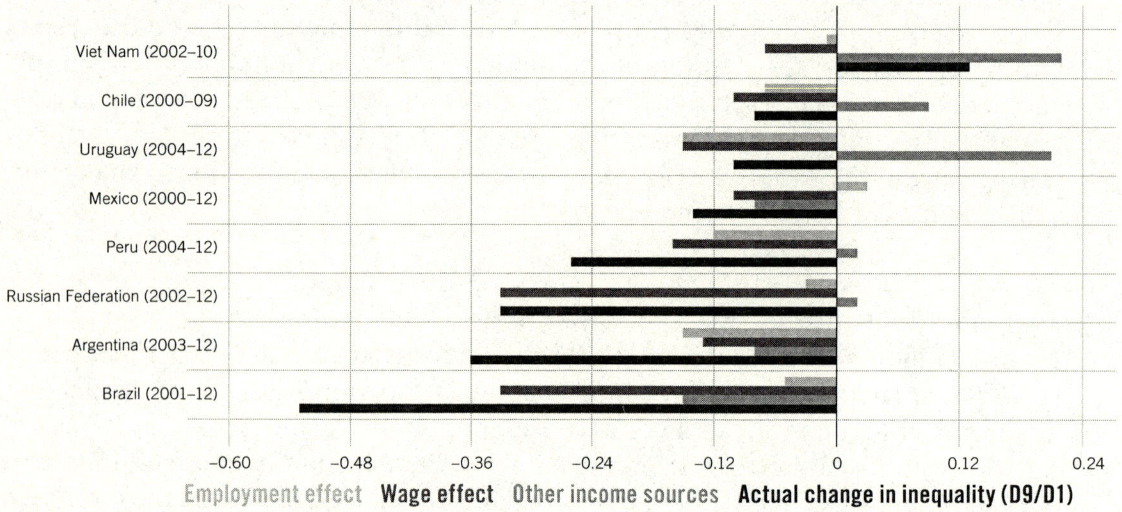

Note: For methodology, definitions and database, see Appendix II.
Source: ILO estimates. Data accessible at: www.ilo.org/gwr-figures

insufficient to bring about an overall reduction in inequality. A similar outcome occurred in South Africa (not shown in figure 27), where the data do not allow for the decomposition exercise to be applied, but where data from other sources show an increase in income inequality (see section 7 above) and a decline in wage inequality.

In those emerging and developing economies where top–bottom inequality declined, middle-class inequality also declined due to the labour market effect. Figure 28 shows the decomposition analysis for middle-class inequality (D7/D3), with countries ranked from top to bottom, from the country where total inequality increased most to that where it declined most. Argentina, Brazil, Peru and the Russian Federation show the greatest declines in inequality within the middle class. In Brazil, the labour market effect accounted for 73 per cent of the fall in middle-class inequality, and in Argentina for 78 per cent. By contrast, in Viet Nam middle-class inequality increased despite a decrease due to the wage effect between 2002 and 2010.

9 Relating inequality to sources of income

To better understand the role of wages in household income, the report next addresses the great variation in the weight of income sources across countries, and across households located at different places in the distribution of income. This is of key importance in order to: (a) understand how recent changes in wages and employment have affected households at different parts of the income distribution, and how this, in turn, has affected income inequality; and (b) develop appropriate policy responses, for example with regard to the mix of minimum wages and transfers. The link between wages and household income is not well documented in the literature, either for developed economies or for emerging and developing economies. This report provides some illustrations of the type of information that policy-makers may find useful in designing policies to address inequality.

9.1 Developed economies: Disaggregating income sources

It is not surprising that, in most developed economies, wages are a major determinant of changes in inequality, given that wages represent about 80 per cent of household income in the United States and about 70 per cent – with some substantial variation between countries – in Europe. Figure 29 provides an estimate of the respective percentages of total household income that, on average, come from wages and from other income sources across a selection of developed economies. In contrast to the previous section, this section disaggregates other income sources, breaking them down into income from self-employment, capital gains, pensions, unemployment benefits, other social transfers and remaining residual income. As pointed out earlier, households where no member is of working age are excluded from the analyses (for sample selection criteria and other aspects of the methodology, see Appendix II). In Germany and Sweden, wages represent at least 75 per cent of household income, whereas in Greece and Italy they account for between 50 and 60 per cent, with self-employment and pensions playing a relatively larger role than in other developed countries.[35] Taken together, pensions, unemployment benefits and other social transfers represent on average between 15 and 20 per cent of household income in both Europe and the United States. In all countries, reported capital gains are a relatively small proportion of reported incomes.[36]

Non-wage income sources are more important for lower earners

We have seen in section 8 that other (non-wage) income sources play a larger role in changes in top–bottom inequality than in respect of middle-class inequality. This reflects the fact that income sources at both the top and the bottom of the income distribution are more diverse than in the middle, where households rely mostly on wages. In figure 30, households are ranked in ascending order by their per capita household income and divided into six groups: the "bottom 10 per cent", the "lower" income group (11th–30th percentiles), the "lower middle" class (31st–50th percentiles), the "upper middle" class (51st–70th percentiles), the "upper"

Figure 29 Share of wages in household income, latest year: Selected developed economies and European average

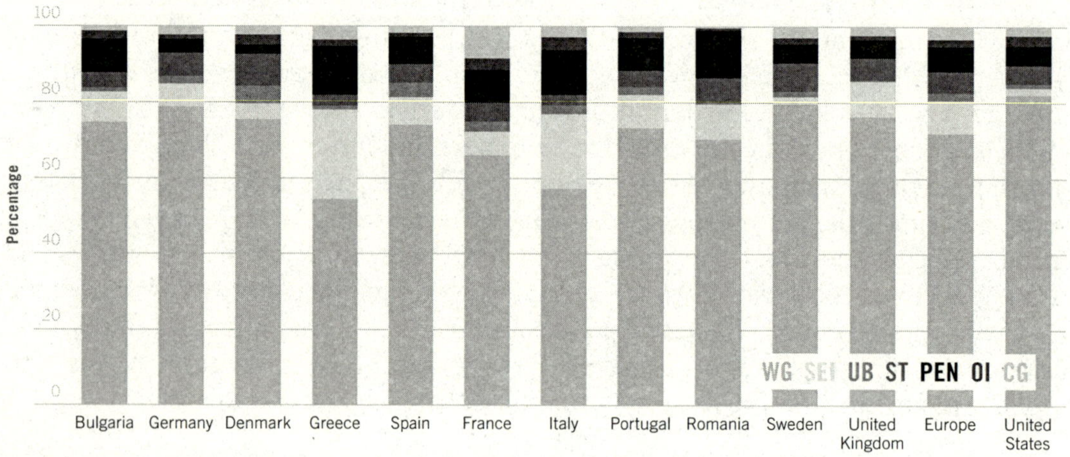

WG = wages; SEI = self-employment income; UB = unemployment benefits; ST = other social transfers; PEN = old-age pensions; OI = residual income; CG= capital gains.

The European average includes: Austria, Belgium, Bulgaria, Cyprus, Czech Republic, Denmark, Estonia, Finland, France, Germany, Greece, Hungary, Iceland, Ireland, Italy, Latvia, Lithuania, Luxembourg, the Netherlands, Norway, Poland, Portugal, Romania, Slovakia, Slovenia, Spain, Sweden and the United Kingdom.

In the case of European economies, *social transfers* include old-age benefits, survivor benefits, sickness benefits, disability benefits and education allowances (aggregated at the household level) and family and/or children allowances, housing allowances as well as social exclusion allowances not elsewhere classified (e.g., incomes for destitute people, drug addicts, alcoholics or victims of criminal violence, among others). The aggregation excludes unemployment benefits and old-age pensions which, for the purpose of illustration, are singled out in the figure. *Old-age benefits* cover benefits that provide a replacement income when the aged person retires from the labour market, or guarantee a certain income when a person has reached a prescribed age (private pension plans are included as part of *capital gains*). *Capital gains* include individual private pension plans, dividends from incorporated business, interest and profits received from capital investment in an unincorporated business in which the person does not work, and income from the rent of property or land. *Residual income* includes regular intra-household transfers (e.g. alimony, child support, cash support from households in other countries), in-kind payments, value of goods produced for own consumption, and income received from family members aged 15 or below with a non-working status.

In the case of the United States, all variables except *residual income* are defined as in the EU-SILC. *Residual income* includes income received from other household members who are neither the head of household nor the spouse of the head (this is the case in about 6 per cent of households). While the data set indicates that this particular income is not from social transfers, it does not indicate whether it is from employment or from capital gains.

Source: ILO estimates; see Appendix II.

income group (71st–90th percentiles) and the "top 10 per cent". As before, these labels are formulated purely for practical purposes, to facilitate the description of results, and do not have a sociological interpretation. For all the selected countries shown in figure 30, it is for the poorest 10 per cent of households that wages represent the smallest source of household income, and in the middle classes and upper-income groups that wages frequently make up the largest source of household income. This pattern can in fact be observed in almost all developed economies.

There is also great variability across countries in the proportion of household income made up by wages in the top and bottom 10 per cent of households. Figure 30 shows, for example, that among the bottom 10 per cent, wages represent about 50 per cent of household income in the United States, more than 30 per in Italy and about 25 per cent in France. By contrast, in the United Kingdom wages represent less than 20 per cent of household income among the poorest households, in Germany less than 10 per cent, and in Romania less than 5 per cent. In all countries, social transfers play an important role in supporting low-income households

Figure 30 Household income by group and source in selected developed economies, latest year

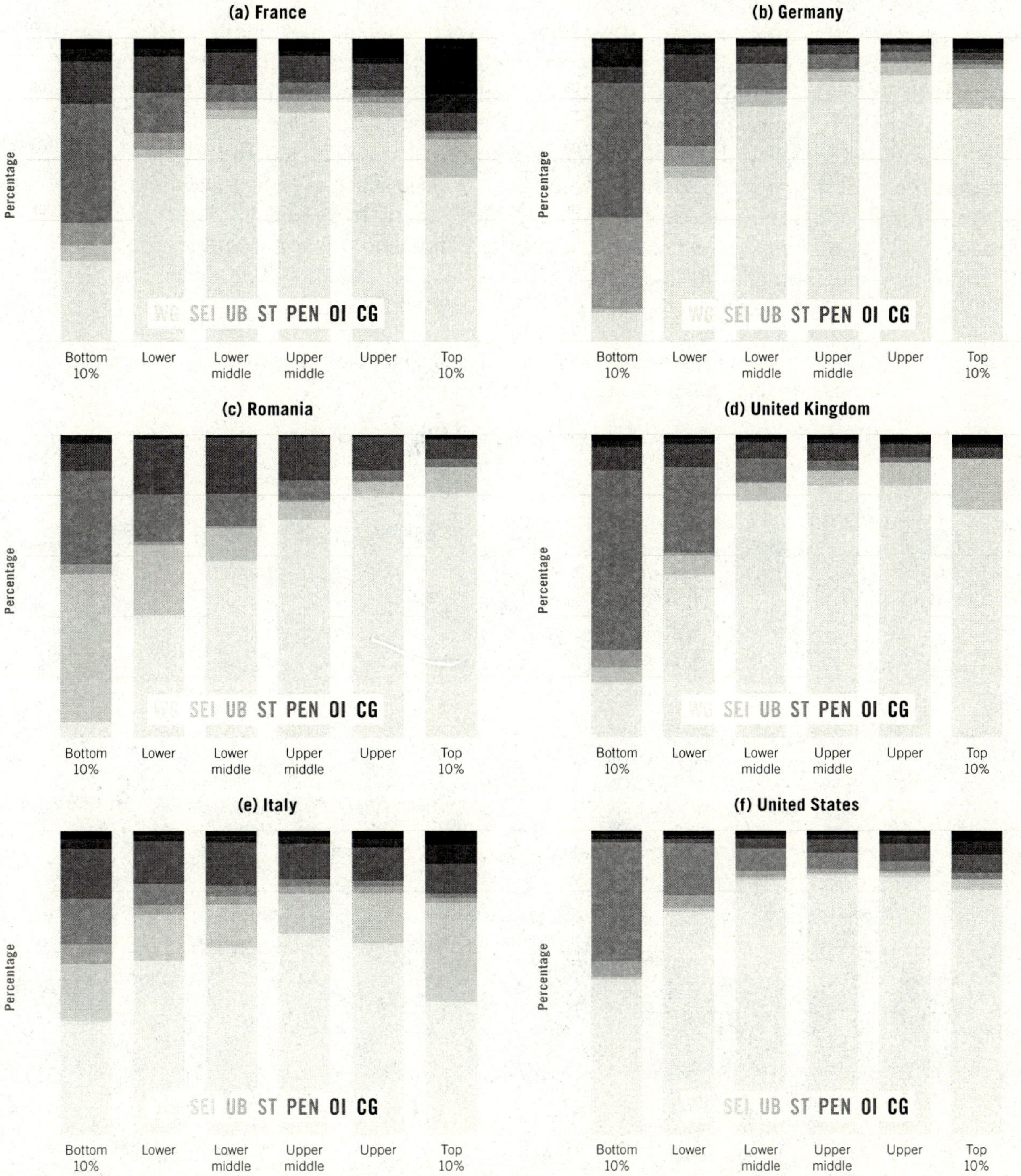

(a)–(d): wages represent less than 30 per cent of household income among the poorest 10 per cent of households.
(e)–(f): wages represent more than 30 per cent of household income among the poorest 10 per cent of households.

WG = wages; SEI = self-employment income; UB = unemployment benefits; ST = other social transfers; PEN = old-age pensions; OI = residual income; CG= capital gains.

Note: "Bottom 10%" reflects up to the first decile; "lower" reflects from above the first decile to the third decile inclusive; "lower middle" reflects from above the third decile to the fifth included; "upper middle" reflects from above the fifth decile and up to the seventh included; "upper" reflects from above the seventh decile to the ninth included; "top 10%" reflects the tenth decile.

Source: ILO estimates.

(as compared with other income groups), even though the type of transfers varies across countries. In Germany, for instance, unemployment benefits and other social transfers play an almost equally important role, whereas in other countries unemployment benefits make up a much smaller share of household income in the bottom 10 per cent.[37] Among the middle and upper classes, wages represent the highest share of household income in almost all countries, reaching about 80 per cent or more in Germany, the United Kingdom and the United States. In Italy and France, the richest 10 per cent of households draw a large share of their household income from income sources other than wages, particularly from self-employment income and capital gains (even though both of these household income sources are likely to be underestimated in household surveys).

Figure 31 Real growth in household income by source of income for the top and bottom 10 per cent, Spain and Romania, 2006–10

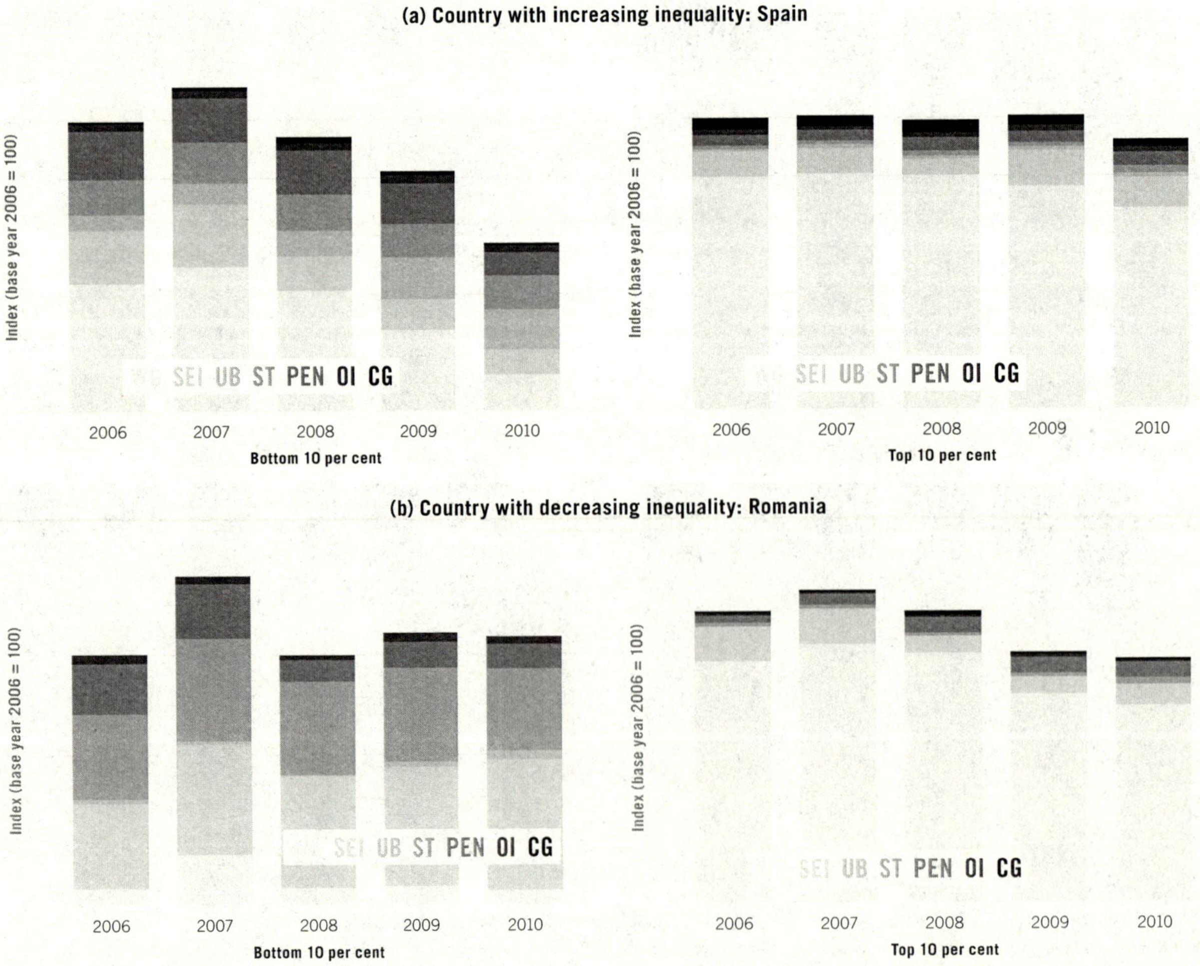

WG = wages; SEI = self-employment income; UB = unemployment benefits; ST = other social transfers; PEN = old-age pensions; OI = residual income; CG= capital gains.

Note: The D9/D1 ratio used in the report cannot be compared to the ratio of the top to the bottom 10 per cent in this figure, since the former is a "threshold measure" and this figure shows averages within deciles.

Source: ILO estimates.

How information on income sources throws light on the sources of inequality

Figure 31 shows the change in income sources in two countries over the period 2006 to 2010 to provide an illustration of why top–bottom inequality (D9/D1) increased in Spain (the country in our sample where inequality rose most) and why it declined in Romania (the country in our sample where inequality declined most, together with Bulgaria). The figure shows the real change (i.e., adjusted for inflation) in household income of the top and bottom 10 per cent, broken down by source of income.

In Spain, growing inequality between 2006 and 2010 is the result of household income falling more in real terms in the bottom 10 per cent than in the top 10 per cent (the overall bars – where 2006 serves as the base year equal to 100 – shrink more for the bottom 10 per cent across time than for the top 10 per cent). Looking at the different components of the bars, we see that the share of household income from wages declined in real terms between 2007 and 2010 for those in the bottom 10 per cent. Incomes from self-employment and from pensions also declined. For the bottom 10 per cent, only income from unemployment benefits increased, but not enough to prevent a sharp decline in overall real income. For the top 10 per cent, household income from wages also declined, but by proportionally less than at the bottom.

Box 6 The largest drop in income inequality in the European Union during the Great Recession: The puzzling case of Romania

Romania registered the largest decrease in income inequality among all EU Member States over the recent recession: a 4.5 point drop in the Gini coefficient between 2007 and 2010. During these years, the country experienced a severe economic downturn and some of the toughest fiscal consolidation measures applied anywhere in the EU, including a 25 per cent wage cut for public sector employees. At the same time, some categories of low-income households saw modest increases in welfare payments. The drop in inequality thus appears to reflect the impact of wage cuts at the top of the income distribution and modest gains for low-income households.

Romania nevertheless remains a country with a high level of income inequality. This is in large part attributable to the gap between wage earners and individuals who are self-employed or contributing family workers. In Romania, self-employed individuals and contributing family workers represent over 90 per cent of employment in agriculture, which itself makes up 29 per cent of total employment – by far the highest level in any EU Member State. The high share of employment in agriculture, and the comparatively high proportion of self-employed and contributing family workers, is a consequence of the slow transition to a market economy. Only 37.5 per cent of individuals living in rural areas are employed, while 34.6 per cent are self-employed and a further 27.3 per cent are contributing family workers. Underemployment in rural areas is also a key driver of economic inequality in Romania, as rural inhabitants mix subsistence farming with various forms of self-employment, informal employment and cyclical employment abroad to supplement their incomes. On average, households draw only 36 per cent of their income from self-employment in agriculture, and 55 per cent from self-employment outside farming.

It should be pointed out that there are methodological difficulties in measuring income inequality in Romania. Unstable and often informal and undeclared forms of income from self-employment are likely to be underreported. To reduce the problem of item non-response, the National Statistical Office imputes these values. This widespread imputation of own production of agricultural products in Romanian household income surveys significantly decreases income inequality indicators.

Source: Domnisoru, 2014.

In Romania, a different story emerges: over the whole period 2006–10, top–bottom inequality declined because household income, in real terms, fell at the top (the overall size of the bar shrank) but increased slightly at the bottom. Looking at the different components, wages accounted for a small proportion of household income in both 2006 and 2010 for households at the bottom: most household income came from self-employment and from social transfers. In Romania, the top 10 per cent rely to a much larger extent on wages, although this source of income has been declining. The fall in inequality in the country may have been due to fiscal consolidation measures affecting the top of the income distribution, including public sector wage cuts, and modest gains, mostly from social transfers, for low-income households (Domnisoru, 2014) (see box 6).

9.2 Emerging and developing economies: A varied and evolving picture

A higher share of self-employment

In emerging and developing economies, the contribution of wages to household income is usually smaller than in developed economies, ranging from about 50–60 per cent in Argentina, Brazil, Chile, Mexico and the Russian Federation (levels similar to Greece or Italy) to about 40 per cent in Peru and 30 per cent in Viet Nam (see figure 32).[38] Conversely, self-employment income generally comprises a larger share of household income than in developed economies, varying from about 10 per cent in the Russian Federation to over 40 per cent in Viet Nam. The lower average share of wages and higher share of self-employment income are a natural reflection of the structural difference in employment status between developed economies and emerging and developing economies: the proportion of employees in total employment is much lower – and the proportion of self-employed workers much higher – in the latter (see figure 14 in Part I). The share of income accounted for by social transfers ranges from about 5 to 20 per cent of household income, although the content differs depending on the country, as explained in the note to the figure.

The share of wages among the bottom 10 per cent of households varies widely in the group of emerging and developing economies shown in figure 33. For this group, wages range from about 50 per cent of household income in the Russian Federation to less than 10 per cent in Viet Nam. The share of wages in middle-income groups is also mixed. In Argentina, Brazil, China and the Russian Federation, the share of wages rises gradually across the middle classes before declining in the highest income groups. By contrast, in South Africa, the share of wages rises sharply among the three higher income groups, with social transfers representing the largest share of income to those in the entire lower half of the distribution.

Strong growth in real wages helps to temper inequality

Contrary to the case of most developed economies, where the context has been one of lower economic growth or persistent recession, the picture is much more dynamic in many of the emerging and developing economies. Among countries where inequality fell, the trend was frequently driven by strong growth in real

Figure 32 Share of wages in household income: Selected emerging and developing economies, latest year*

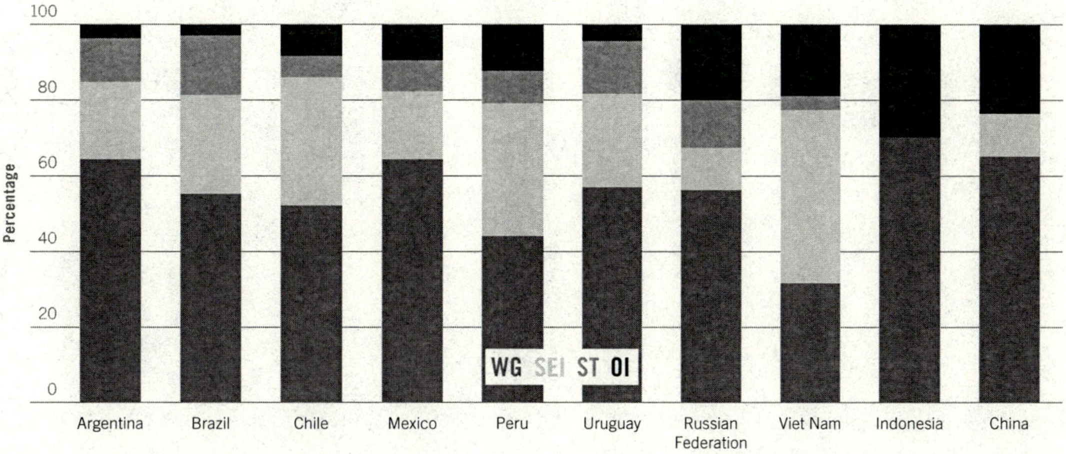

WG = wages; SEI = self-employment labour income; ST = social transfers; OI = other income.

Note: In the case of emerging and developing economies, *self-employment income* includes gains from employment as either self-employed or own-account worker with employees. Whereas for the self-employed (employer) in developed economies it is possible to distinguish between "income from labour" and their profits, this is not the case for emerging and developing economies: in this case, the reported self-employment is likely to include profits generated by their self-employment (own account) business. *Social transfers* are defined for each economy as described below in detail. *Other income* includes in-kind payments, *capital gains*, incomes received by family members aged 15 or below with a non-working status and the difference between the sum of income of all individual household members and the total income reported for the household in the data set. *Capital gains* are included as part of *other income* for emerging and developing economies because they cannot be distinguished from *other income* sources.

In the case of Indonesia, the data do not allow for a distinction between self-employment income and social transfers. In the case of China, social transfers cannot be identified as a unique category by the data and are therefore likely to be included in "other income sources". See note 38 with reference to China's social transfers as described in ILO, 2014f.

In the Russian Federation and Viet Nam, the data cannot uniquely isolate statutory pensions and unemployment benefits. Therefore, social transfers refer to all incomes from the public social protection system including statutory pensions and unemployment benefits.

In all the Latin American countries represented in the figure (Argentina, Brazil, Chile, Mexico, Peru and Uruguay), social transfers are the sum of all incomes from the public social protection system (including unemployment benefits, statutory old age pensions and all other non-contributory social benefits) as well as benefits from private institutions (e.g., benefits received from religious institutions as is explicitly in the data for Argentina).

* See Appendix III for a definition of the dates and data sources.

Source: ILO estimates based on national sources.

household income and especially by real wages at the bottom. This can be observed in figure 34, which shows the real change (i.e. adjusted for inflation) of household incomes of the top and bottom 10 per cent, broken down by source of income, for selected emerging and developing economies. In the case of Brazil, between 2001 and 2012 real wages of the bottom 10 per cent increased more than those of the top 10 per cent; social transfers and other income sources also increased considerably (in real terms) during that period at the bottom of the distribution. In the Russian Federation as well, the decline in total inequality between 2002 and 2012 took place in a context of much more rapidly increasing household incomes, with social transfers growing much more at the bottom than at the top, and wages increasing more at the bottom since 2006.

Income inequality may increase even where wage inequality falls

In some countries, inequality increased in spite of lower wage inequality. In the case of Viet Nam, the share of wages in household income of those at the bottom of the income distribution appears to have declined, with increases in household

Figure 33 Household income by group and source in selected emerging and developing economies, latest year

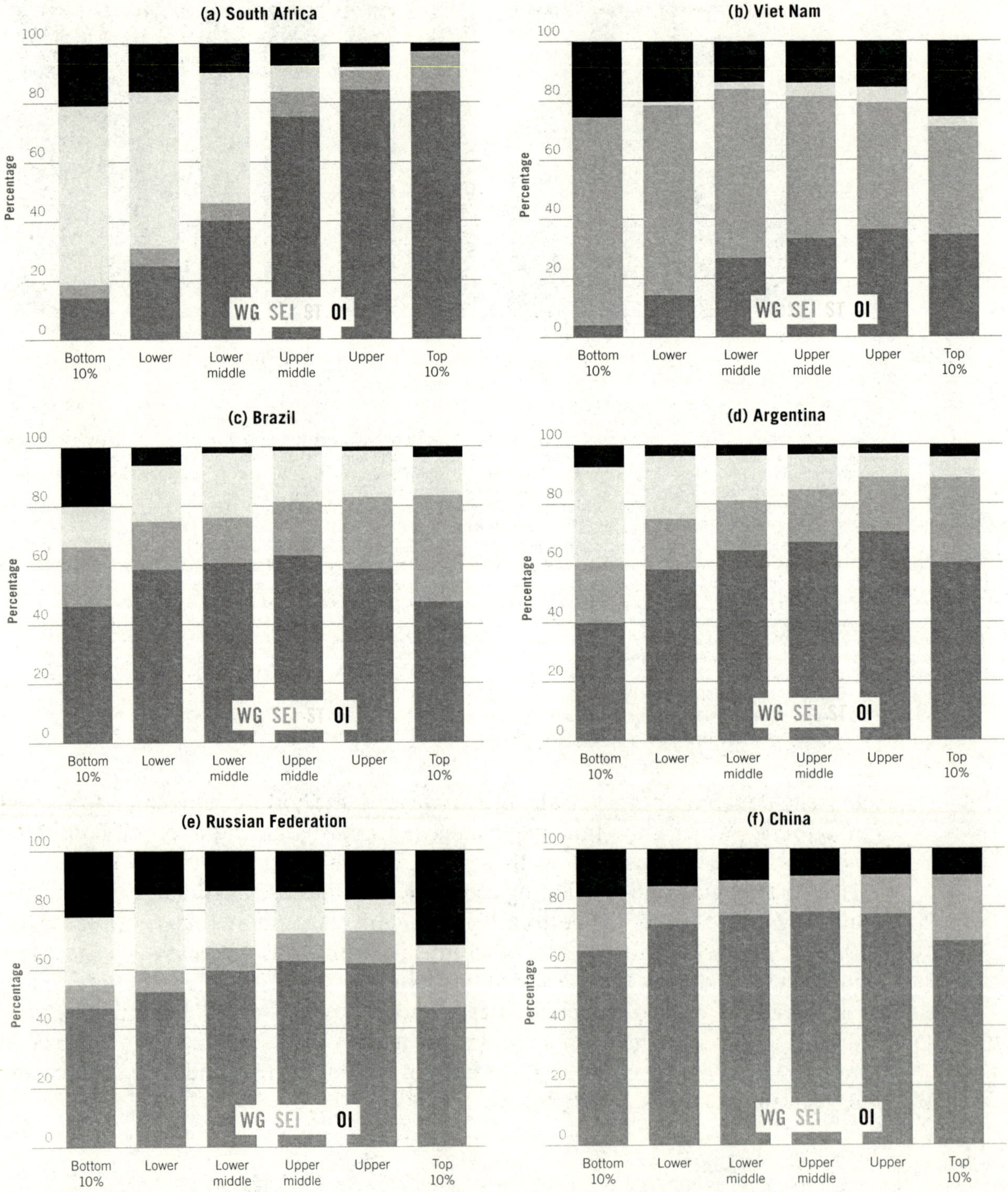

(a)–(b): wages represent less than 30 per cent of household income among the poorest 10 per cent of households.
(c)–(f): wages represent more than 30 per cent of household income among the poorest 10 per cent of households.

WG = wages; SEI = self-employment labour income; ST = social transfers; OI = other income.

Source: ILO estimates.

Figure 34 Real growth in household income by income source for the top and bottom 10 per cent, selected emerging and developing economies, 2001/02 to 2010–12

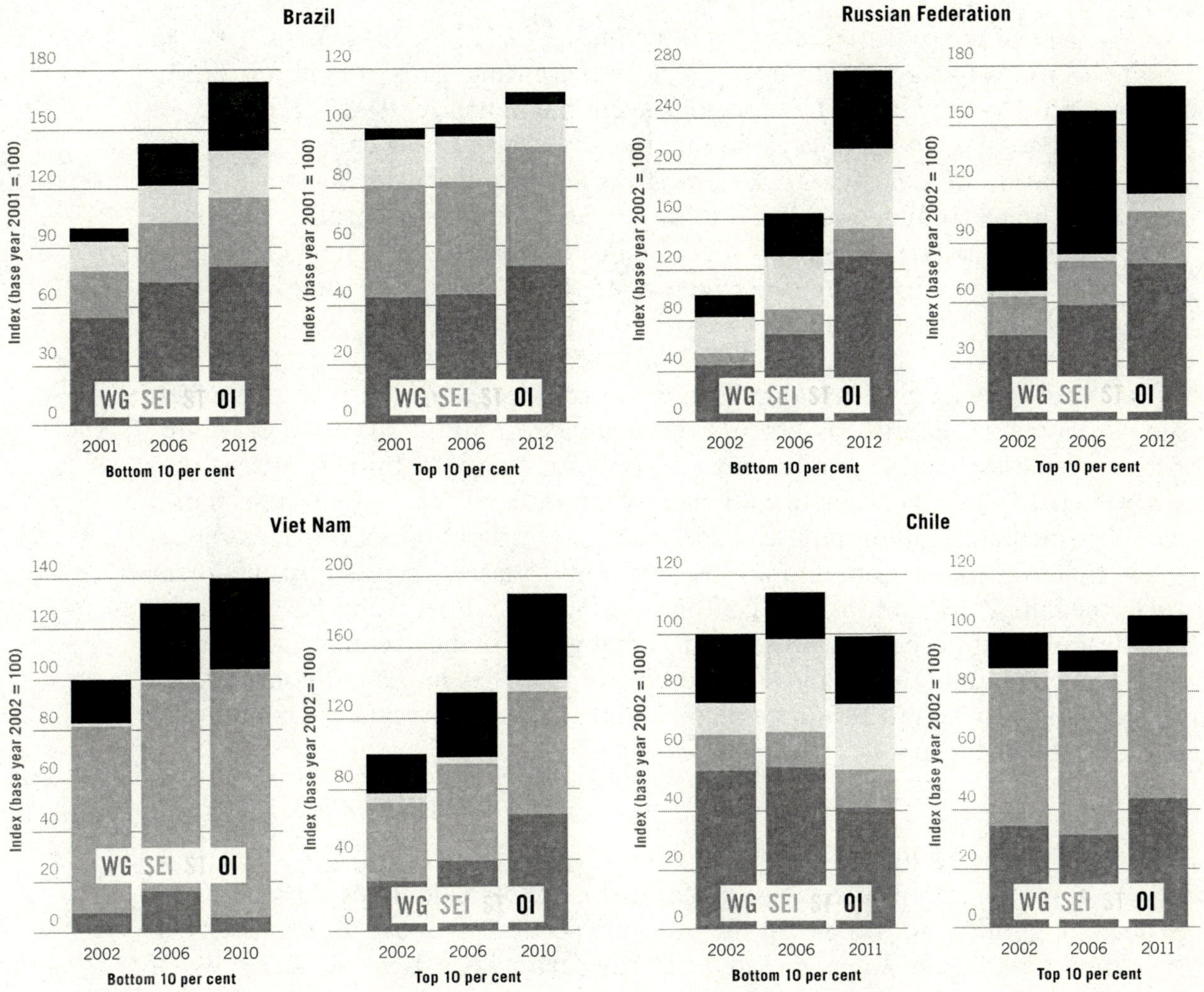

WG = wages; SEI = self-employment labour income; ST = social transfers; OI = other income.

Note: The D9/D1 ratio used in the report cannot be compared to the ratio of the top to the bottom 10 per cent in this figure, since the former is a "threshold measure" and the present figure shows averages within deciles.

Source: ILO estimates.

incomes depending instead on rising income from self-employment and other income sources. One possible explanation might be that those with income from wages have moved up to a higher income group on the income ladder, leaving a growing share of self-employment income as a percentage of household income in the bottom 10 per cent. Given the lower proportion of wage earners than in developed economies, income inequality in emerging and developing economies is linked not only with wage inequality among paid employees, but also to a large extent with the gap between wages and income from self-employment. In Chile, inequality clearly diminished between 2002 and 2006, as transfers to the poorest households increased, but increased between 2006 and 2011 as wages fell at the bottom.

10 Wage gaps: Which workers earn less than others, and why?

One element of the overall level of total inequality lies in the wage gaps between different groups of workers. In order to close these wage gaps, it is important to understand why they exist. The previous section emphasized the importance of wages as a component of household income and showed how changes in wages drive changes in total inequality. However, the varying characteristics of workers across the household income distribution are also important because, although some inequality can be explained with reference to general economy-wide factors, such as returns to education, other factors are more specific to the groups that cluster at the lower end of the wage distribution.

In this final section of Part II, special attention is devoted to groups which often experience discrimination or other disadvantages in the labour market, such as women, migrant workers and those who work in the informal economy. Although labour market institutions and policies such as minimum wages that aim to benefit all workers can be designed to cover all paid employees in principle, reducing inequality often requires additional targeted policy action. This report shows that women, migrants and workers in the informal economy sometimes incur "wage penalties" for multiple and complex reasons that differ from one country to another, and that the penalty occurs at different places in the overall wage distribution. Understanding the reasons for these wage penalties in the national context, and adopting policies to eliminate them, could make a significant contribution to reducing income inequality.

Women, migrants, and informal workers

To illustrate the importance of wage gaps, this report calculates these gaps for women, migrants, and workers in the informal economy, across the earnings distribution. Unadjusted wage gaps refer to the earnings of men, or nationals, or formal economy workers, respectively (at a given percentile in the wage distribution), minus the earnings of women, or migrants, or informal economy workers (at the same percentile in the distribution). The unadjusted gaps are then decomposed into an "explained" and an "unexplained" part. The explained part takes into account: experience; education (grouped into four categories); occupational category (managerial, high-skilled, semi-skilled, low-skilled and unskilled); economic activity (about ten categories, including manufacturing, services, and public administration), location (urban, rural); and work intensity (hours worked). When experience is missing, age is considered as a proxy since education is also included in the specification. The unexplained part – or wage penalty – is what remains after adjusting for these observable labour market characteristics, which should in principle explain pay differences.[39] The full methodology is explained in Appendix IV.

From a policy standpoint, both the explained and unexplained components are important as channels through which to redress differences in pay across groups. From the onset, the heterogeneous nature of these groups should be emphasized and accordingly, appropriate policy responses vary. The drivers of both the explained and unexplained components may overlap. In particular, the unexplained component may capture discriminatory practices that can also influence variables considered in the explained component.[40]

10.1 The gender wage gap

Much research has attempted to interpret the gender wage gap, and the factors that have been advanced by researchers include: (1) an undervaluation of women's work; (2) workplace characteristics (e.g. how substitutable workers are for each other, the value of face time, etc.); (3) sex segregation channelling women into low value added jobs; (4) the overall wage structure in a country – which may be shaped by wage-setting mechanisms that may have been designed with a focus on workers in male-dominated sectors); (5) the view of women as economic dependants; and (6) the likelihood that women are in unorganized sectors or not represented in unions (Goldin, 2014; Chen, Ge, Lai and Wan, 2013; Grimshaw, 2011; Rubery, Grimshaw and Figueiredo, 2005; Heinze and Wolf, 2010; Rubery, 2003). Family behavioural patterns may also influence the gap (see box 7 on the motherhood wage gap).

Unexplained factors remain important

Figure 36 shows the gender wage gap, calculated for each decile of the wage distribution and split into an explained and unexplained component, for selected countries. Wage earners are ranked according to their level of wages, from the lowest decile to the highest. The total unadjusted wage gap is the sum of the two bars: the dark bar represents the proportion of the wage gap which can be explained by observable labour market characteristics, and the light bar is the "unexplained" gap. The gaps are provided in absolute values: for example, in the first decile in Belgium there is an unadjusted gender wage gap of about €400, whereas in Estonia it is about €50. The shapes of the decompositions vary across countries and across groups. In Belgium and Estonia, women receive lower wages than men throughout the distribution, but the unexplained part of the gap tends to be higher among better-paid women. In the United States, the unexplained part is proportionally small, and affects predominantly better-paid women. In Peru and Viet Nam, the explained part tends to increase at higher wage levels of the wage distribution. By contrast, in Sweden the unadjusted gender wage gap is very small (the light and dark bars generally offset each other; the negative dark bars imply that women would actually earn more than men if discrimination and other unexplained factors did not exist). A similar situation can be observed in Chile and in the Russian Federation, where discrimination and other unexplained factors alone account for differences in pay between men and women.

Figure 37 presents (1) the level of the average gender wage gap at the national level for the countries included (the dark bar) and (2) a counterfactual estimate of the contribution of the unexplained part of the wage gap to the overall unadjusted wage gap (the light bar). The counterfactual wage gap is the gap which would exist if men and women were equally remunerated entirely according to the observable labour market characteristics taken into account in this report (i.e. education,

Box 7 The motherhood wage gap

What is the motherhood wage gap?

The motherhood wage gap measures the wage gap between mothers and non-mothers, the latter being defined in most econometric studies as women without dependent children. This is different from the gender wage gap, which measures the wage gap between all women and all men in the workforce. While there is a considerable international literature on the motherhood gap, differences both in methodologies and in definitions of mothers and non-mothers create difficulties in comparing estimates. Moreover, in many countries, the data are often unsuitable for analysis, typically because the questions posed in surveys make it difficult to establish a child's mother or father (particularly in developing countries where the nuclear family is less common). Nevertheless, many studies draw on international harmonized pay and employment data that provide a useful basis for cross-country comparison, and others provide informative trend analyses for single countries. Data on the motherhood wage gap are provided below for a selection of countries; however, the figures are not directly comparable, for the reasons just mentioned.

From the available research, it appears that the unadjusted motherhood gap tends to be larger in developing countries than in developed countries. Globally, the motherhood gap increases with the number of children a woman has; in many European countries, for example, having one child has only a small negative effect, but women with two and especially three children experience a significant wage penalty. In developing countries, evidence suggests that the gender of the child may matter, as daughters may be more likely than sons to help with household and caring tasks, thereby reducing the motherhood gap. Whether the wage penalty associated with motherhood accumulates over time also varies from one country to another. For example, in some countries, mothers who have a strong job attachment are found to experience a wage decrease immediately on return to employment, but soon catch up with non-mothers. In short, while the existence of a motherhood gap seems universal, the magnitude of the effect that motherhood has on wages varies from country to country.

Explanations for the motherhood wage gap

The main reasons advanced for the motherhood wage gap arise in different analytical frameworks.

An *economics* approach tends to emphasize: (1) reduced "human capital", or knowledge, arising from employment interruptions or reductions in working time, and possible lessened tendency to seek out training or higher-paid positions with more responsibility; and (2) employment in family-friendly jobs, such as some part-time positions, which are typically not as well paid. A *sociological* approach tends to emphasize that: (1) employers may make hiring and promotion decisions based on stereotypical expectations of the burdens imposed by families on mothers' time and energy; (2) the undersupply or affordability of childcare and other work–family accommodations are a frequent concern; and (3) female-dominated occupations and workplaces tend to be less rewarded than male-dominated occupations due to undervaluation of women's work. A *comparative institutionalist* approach emphasizes that: (1) countries provide very different opportunities for mothers to access jobs with higher wages through specific policies (e.g. childcare provision, maternity and paternity leave); (2) a country's tax and benefit system may confer tax advantages on mothers who are identified as economically dependent; (3) the size of the motherhood wage gap varies with the degree of inequality in a country's overall wage structure; (4) the cultural and family context matters, especially in countries with less developed policy interventions; and (5) there may be implementation gaps, where protective or non-discrimination policies exist but are not enforced or observed, for example in the informal sector or under non-regular employment arrangements in the formal sector.

Figure 35 Motherhood wage gap in selected emerging and developing economies, latest year

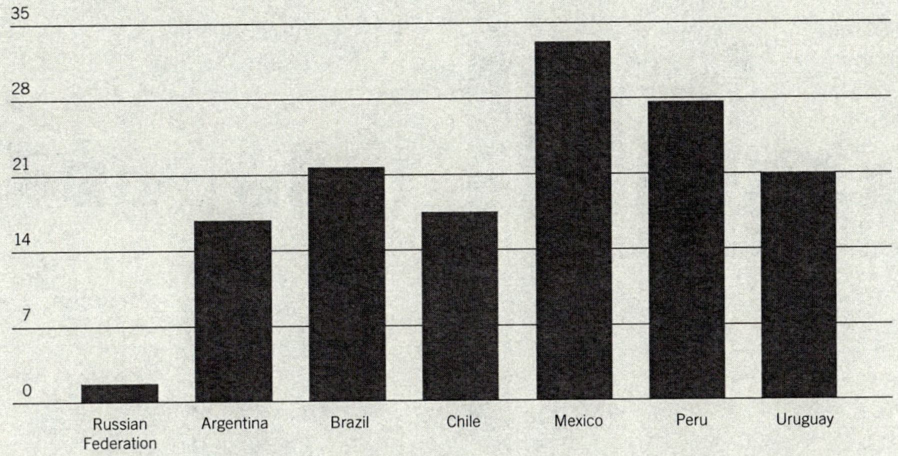

Note: The motherhood wage gap is defined as MPG = ((Enm – Em) ÷ Enm) × 100, where Enm is the average gross monthly earnings of women who are not mothers and Em is the average gross monthly earnings of mothers.

Source: ILO estimates on trends in the motherhood wage gap. Data accessible at: www.ilo.org/gwr-figures

How to address the motherhood wage gap

The magnitude of the motherhood wage gap and the relevance of some of the abovementioned explanations depend on the constellation of work–family laws, policies and measures, labour market institutions, gender stereotypes and societal expectations in a given country. Nonetheless, there are some general policy recommendations that can be used to address it:

- Job-protected parental leave of adequate duration and with income-related pay funded by social insurance or public funds for both women and men, with specific provision for fathers.
- Accessibility of affordable and quality childcare services and flexible working arrangements for all workers.
- Tax and benefit rules that treat mothers as economically independent adults.
- Addressing the implementation gap in work–family and social policies.
- Preventing and eliminating discrimination based on maternity and family responsibilities and creating a family-friendly workplace culture.
- The right to regulated and flexible working hours, including the upgrading of part-time jobs and access to them for women and men.

Source: Grimshaw and Rubery, forthcoming.

experience, economic activity, location, work intensity and occupation). Once these adjustments are taken into account, in our sample of developed economies (figure 37(a)) the mean gender wage gap nearly disappears (e.g. Austria, Iceland, Italy) or even reverses (e.g. Lithuania, Slovenia, Sweden) in about half the countries in the sample. It declines substantially in other countries but remains largely explained in Germany and the United States. Among our sample of emerging and developing economies (see figure 37(b)), the gender wage gap reverses in Brazil and the Russian Federation. In all other countries in the sample, the wage gap declines substantially, though less so in Argentina and Peru, where much of the

Figure 36 Explained and unexplained gender wage gaps in selected countries, latest year

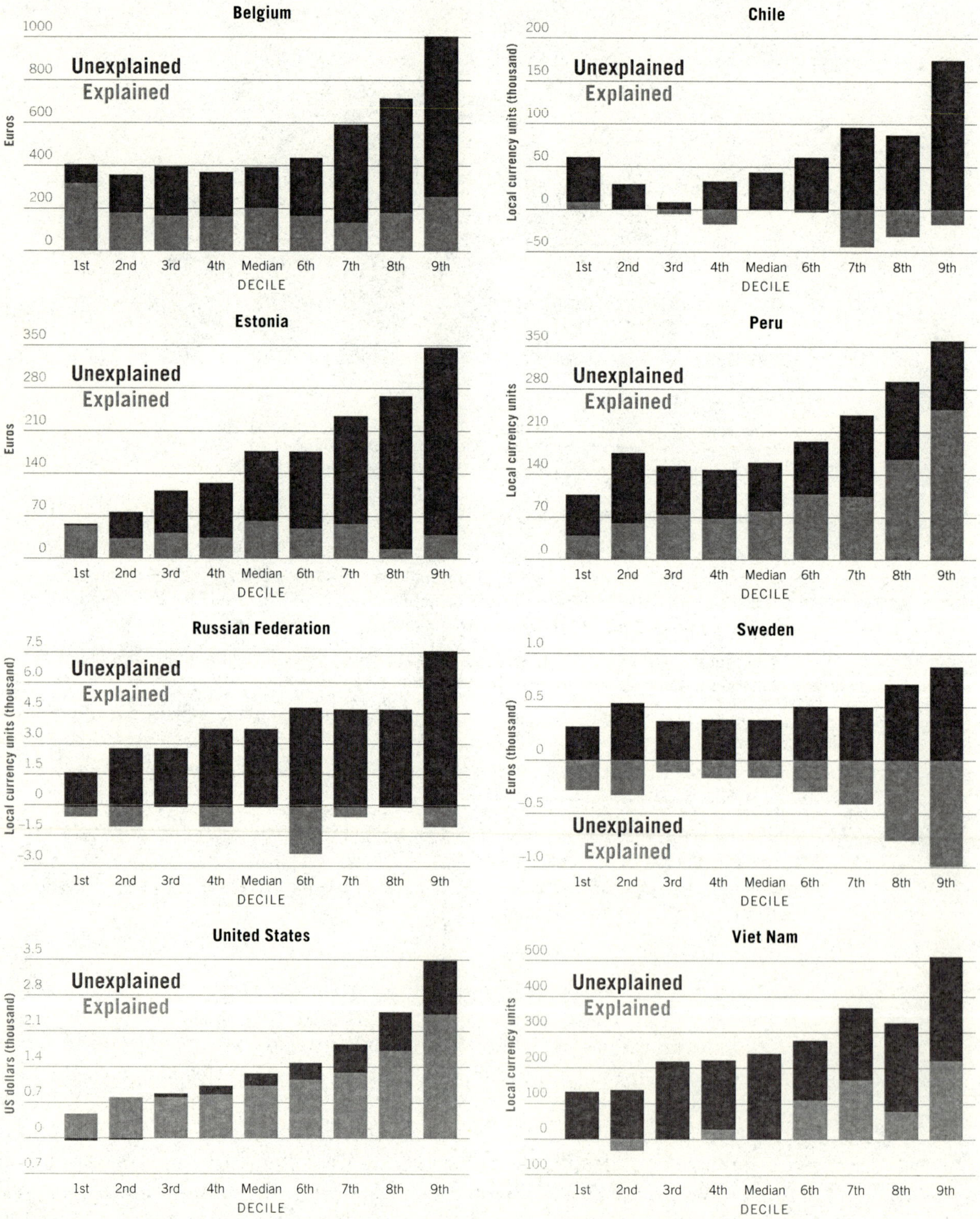

Note: In Europe in 2010, the bottom 10 per cent of women earned about €100 per month less than the bottom 10 per cent of men. Conversely, the top 10 per cent of high-earning women earned close to €700 per month less than the top 10 per cent of men.

Source: ILO estimates.

Figure 37 Eliminating the unexplained gender wage penalty: Mean wage gap before and after adjustment in selected economies, latest year: (a) developed economies; (b) emerging and developing economies

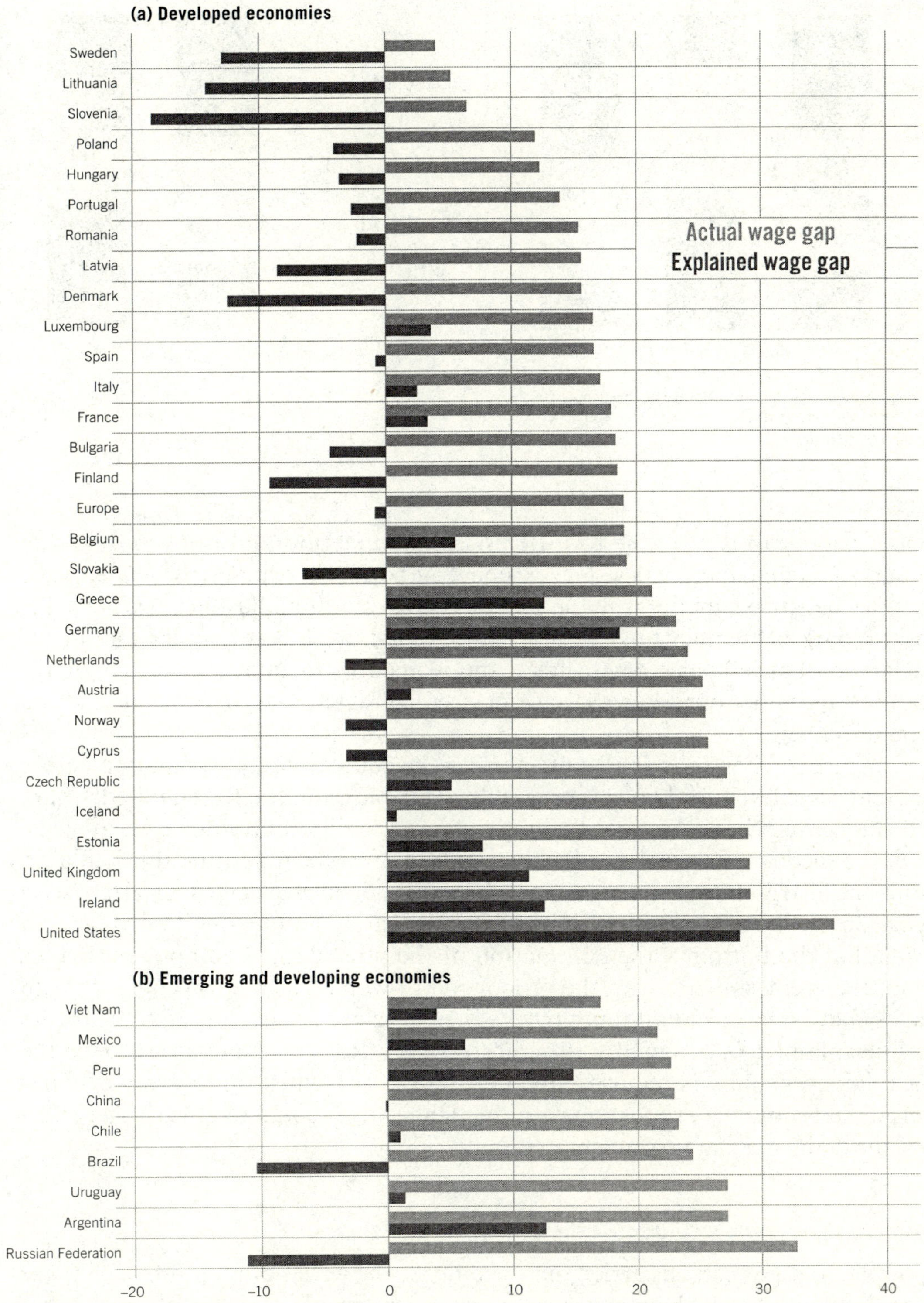

Source: ILO estimates. Data accessible at: www.ilo.org/gwr-figures

Figure 38 Wage distribution and counterfactual wage distribution, Russian Federation and United States, latest year

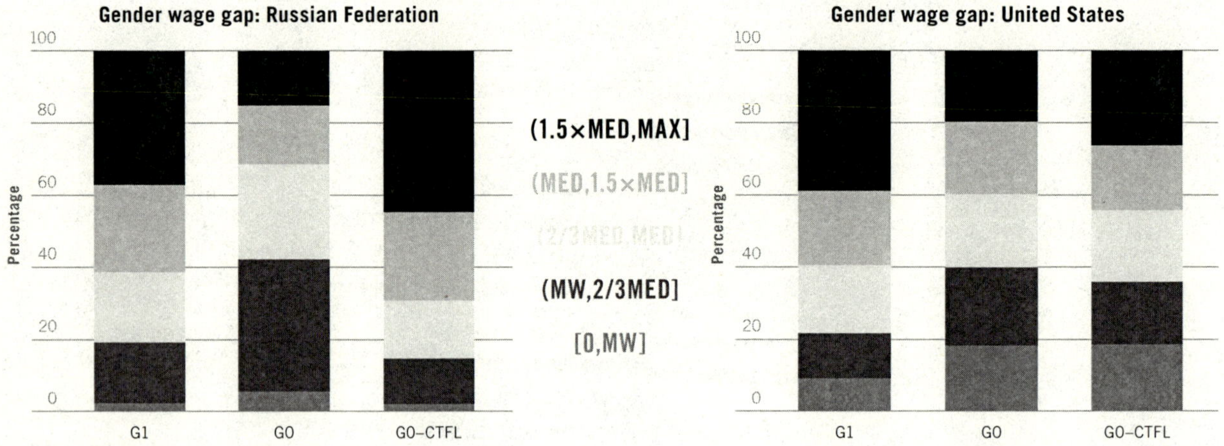

G1: Wage distribution for males; G0: Wage distribution for females; G0-CTFL: Wage distribution for females once the unexplained component is eliminated and the gap is fully described by the explained component.
Source: ILO estimates.

gender wage gap is also due to differences in education and other observable labour market characteristics. The existence of negative "explained" gender wage gaps (i.e. negative light bars), in the presence of positive unadjusted wage gaps (i.e. positive dark bars), points to the importance of gaining a better understanding of the factors that influence pay for men and women with equal experience, qualifications and other observable labour market characteristics, in order to address them effectively.

Figure 38 shows the results of applying the counterfactual estimation across different wage levels for two countries with available data, the Russian Federation and the United States. The first column shows the distribution of men by wage level, the second column shows the distribution of women, and the third column shows the distribution of women absent the unexplained wage gap. Consistent with figure 36 – which showed that in the United States the unexplained wage gap is small at the bottom – the elimination of the unexplained component brings about the greatest increase in the proportion of women in the top category with wages above one and a half times the median wage (where, according to figure 38, the unexplained wage penalty is highest). In the Russian Federation, once the unexplained penalty is removed, the percentage of women on low pay declines considerably, and the proportion earning higher wages equal to at least one and a half times the median wage increases.

10.2 The migrant wage gap

A similar analysis can be carried out to compare the wages of migrants with those of national workers. There are many reasons why wages of migrants may differ from those of nationals, including the fact that their personal characteristics, such

Figure 39 Explained and unexplained migrant–national wage gaps in selected countries, latest year

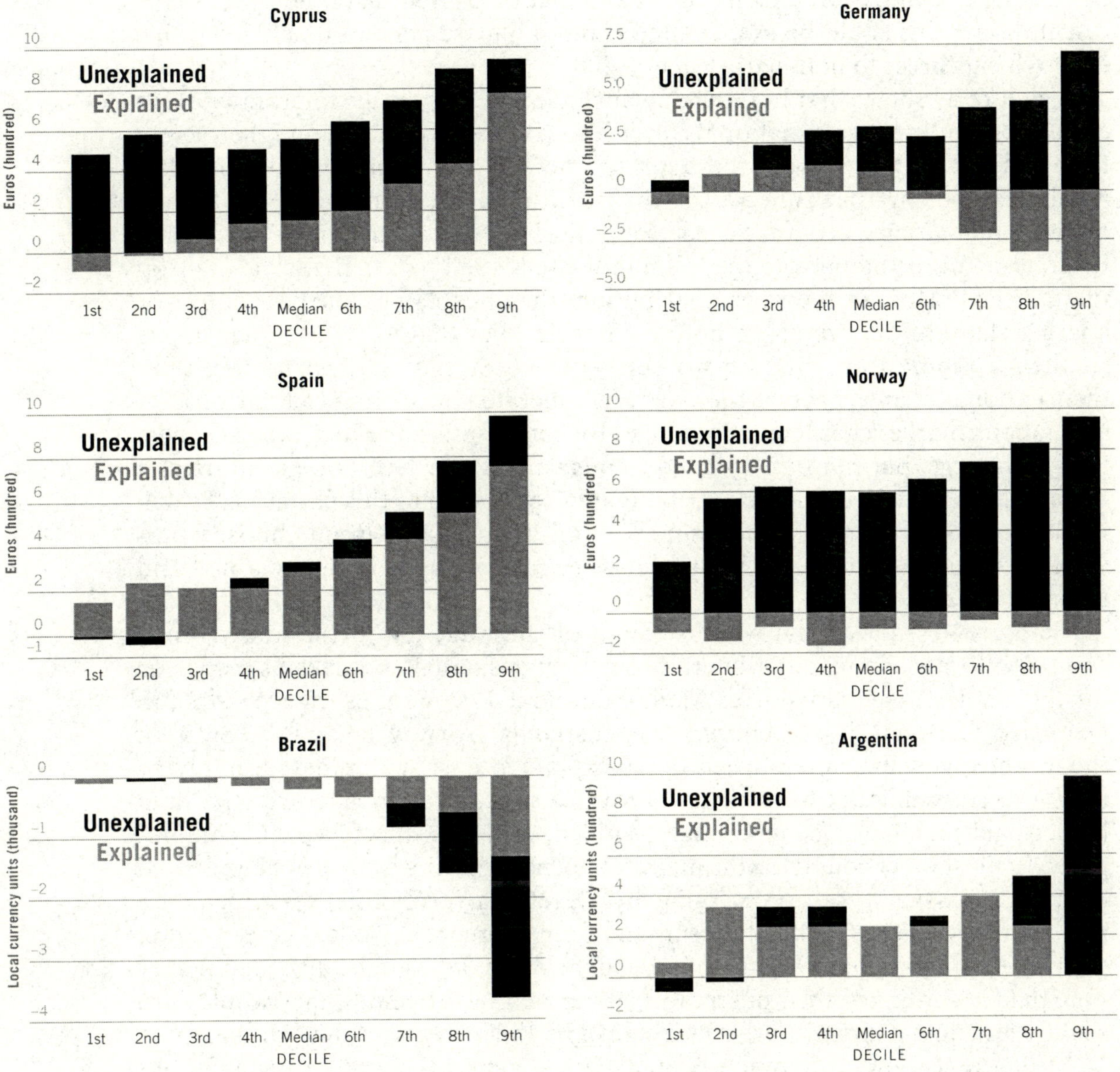

Source: ILO estimates.

as skill level, may advantage or disadvantage them in their country of destination. Part of the gap is also unexplained. Employer discrimination against migrants because of factors such as prejudice or distrust may account for part of the unexplained wage gap (Solé and Parella, 2003). Some research also attributes this to differences in returns to foreign-acquired education; employers may not be sure of the quality of the education acquired abroad (Barrett, McGuinness and O'Brien, 2012). Migrants, particularly single migrants, may also receive lower wages than nationals if they are perceived as having lower income needs than their national counterparts with families to support (Rubery, 2003). In other cases, migrants may be under- or unrepresented through collective representation structures because of difficulties organizing or because nationals dominate the overall representation – this could be exacerbated if migrants are perceived as a low-wage employment threat to nationals (Rubery, 2003).

Figure 39 shows that in Germany, for example, high-wage migrant workers earn less than high-wage nationals, even though they would earn higher wages than nationals if they were remunerated according to their labour market attributes (the dark bar is negative). In Argentina as well, the wage gap among migrant and national top wage earners is exclusively due to the unexplained part. In Cyprus, even though the overall unadjusted wage gap is higher at the top than at the bottom of the wage distribution, the unexplained part accounts for a larger share of the gap at the bottom. This implies that while the wage gap is smaller at the bottom, migrant workers at the bottom would earn more than their national counterparts if they were remunerated according to their observable labour market characteristics alone. By contrast, among high wage earners the gap is large, but can be attributed to migrants' lower levels of education and other observable labour market attributes. One exception to this pattern is Brazil, where according to the available survey data, high-wage migrants (mostly university graduates) earn more than high-wage nationals for both explained and unexplained reasons.

Figure 40 shows what would remain of the wage gap if the unexplained component were eliminated using the same counterfactual approach as employed for the gender wage gap above. Among developed economies (figure 40(a)), in Denmark, Germany, Luxembourg, the Netherlands, Norway, Poland and Sweden, the mean wage gap reverses when the unexplained part is eliminated, implying that on average migrant workers may have more education or experience, work in higher-paid regions, or be more highly skilled, etc., than their national counterparts. In most other countries, the migration penalty declines but is not eliminated after the adjustment. In the emerging and developing economies for which data permit analysis (figure 40(b)), the results are similar, except in Chile. There, migrant workers earn more than their national counterparts on average, although if they were paid according to their observable labour market attributes, they would earn slightly less than national workers (as shown by the increase in the light bar).

Figure 41 shows the counterfactual applied across the wage distribution for two countries, Cyprus and Spain. The first column shows the wage distribution of national employees, whereas the second column presents the same information for migrant employees. The third column shows how migrants would be distributed in these groups if the "unexplained" wage gap were eliminated. We see that in Cyprus, migrant workers are heavily represented in the lowest wage groups.[41] However, this picture changes significantly once the unexplained wage penalty is removed, with the migrant wage distribution becoming more similar to the national wage distribution. This is consistent with figure 37(a), which shows the unexplained component contributing more to the wage gap at the bottom of the wage distribution. By contrast, the corresponding changes in Spain are smaller because most of the wage gap between migrants and nationals is explained by a difference in observable factors.

Figure 40 Eliminating the unexplained migrant wage penalty: Mean wage gap before and after adjustment in selected economies, latest year

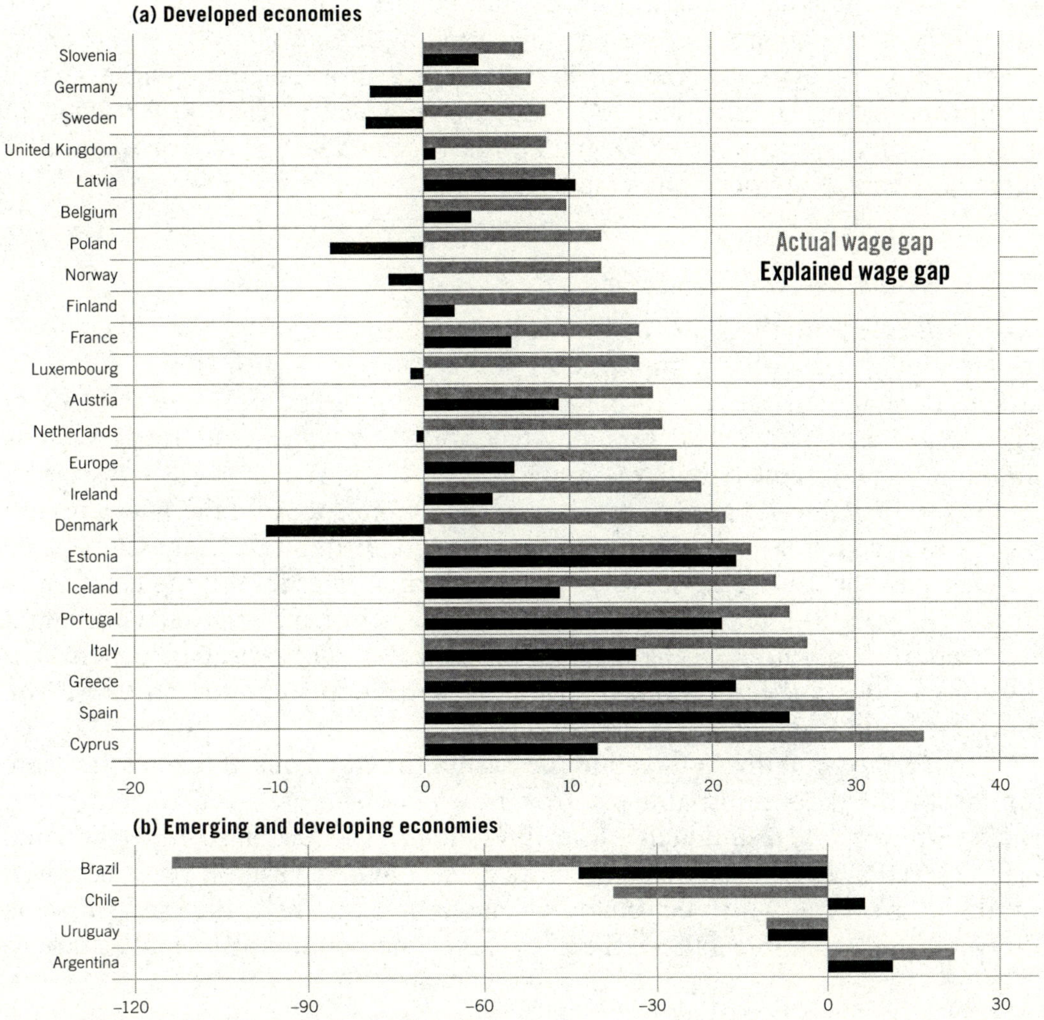

Source: ILO estimates. Data accessible at: www.ilo.org/gwr-figures

Figure 41 Wage distribution and counterfactual wage distribution, Cyprus and Spain, latest year

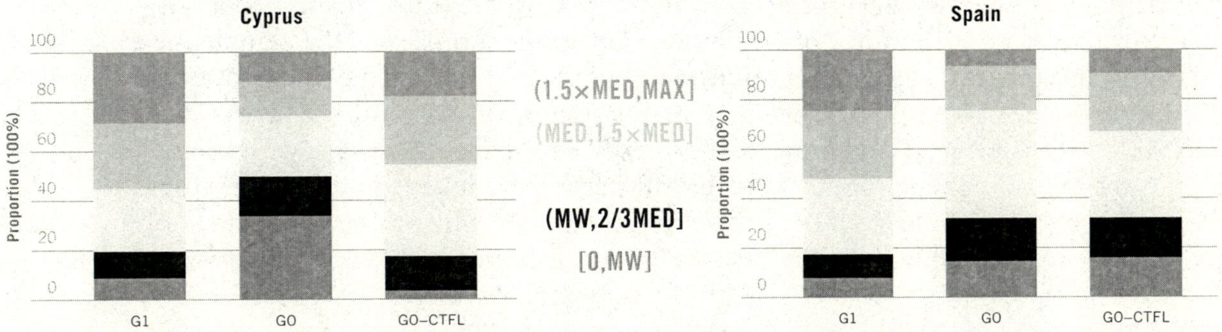

G1: Wage distribution for nationals, GO: Wage distribution for migrants, GO-CTFL: Wage distribution for migrants once the unexplained component is eliminated and the gap is fully described by the explained component.

Source: ILO estimates.

10.3 The informal economy wage gap

Analysing informal economy wage gaps is complex, not least because there are so many different situations and phenomena that can fall into the broad category of the "informal economy". From a statistical point of view, *informal employment* includes both employment in the informal *sector* and informal employment outside the informal sector.[42] In practice, workers in the informal economy differ widely in terms of income, status in employment, sector, type and size of enterprise, and/or degree of coverage by social and employment protection.

The role of segmentation and profitability

Wage gaps affecting those in the informal economy may arise for a variety of reasons, but one common assumption is the existence of some form of labour market segmentation between formal and informal jobs (see box 8 on the case of Argentina). Formal sector workers may be covered by wage regulations, such as minimum wages or collective bargaining provisions and social protection systems to which informal workers may not have access, either because the relevant laws do not cover them or are not effectively enforced. For example, a recent study using household and labour force surveys for 11 emerging and developing economies showed that one-third of employees who were in principle entitled to the minimum wage were in fact paid less; the proportion paid less is also higher for females, ethnic minorities, and for workers in the informal economy and rural areas (Rani, Belser, Oelz and Ranjbar, 2013).

Another explanation is linked to the profitability of firms: if formal firms are more profitable than informal firms, then they may be more likely to share their profits with workers, resulting in a wage premium in the formal sector (Rand and Torm, 2012). Part of the gap may therefore be eliminated through general as well as tailored measures which facilitate "formalization", namely, the incorporation of workers and economic units of the informal economy into the formal economy.

Eliminating the unexplained gap is only part of the solution

Figure 42 shows wage gaps affecting workers in the informal economy for selected Latin American countries. The observable labour market characteristics of informal economy workers differ from those of workers in the formal economy across all points of the wage distribution and for all countries in the sample (i.e. there is an explained gap across the entire distribution). At the same time, however, the unexplained part of the wage gap remains significant. In some countries, such as Argentina (see box 8) and Mexico, the unexplained part of the wage gap is larger than the explained part for most deciles. In Peru, the explained and unexplained components contribute to the wage gap about equally, while in Uruguay most of the wage gap is attributable to workers' observable labour market characteristics.

Figure 42 Explained and unexplained informality wage gaps in selected Latin American countries, latest year

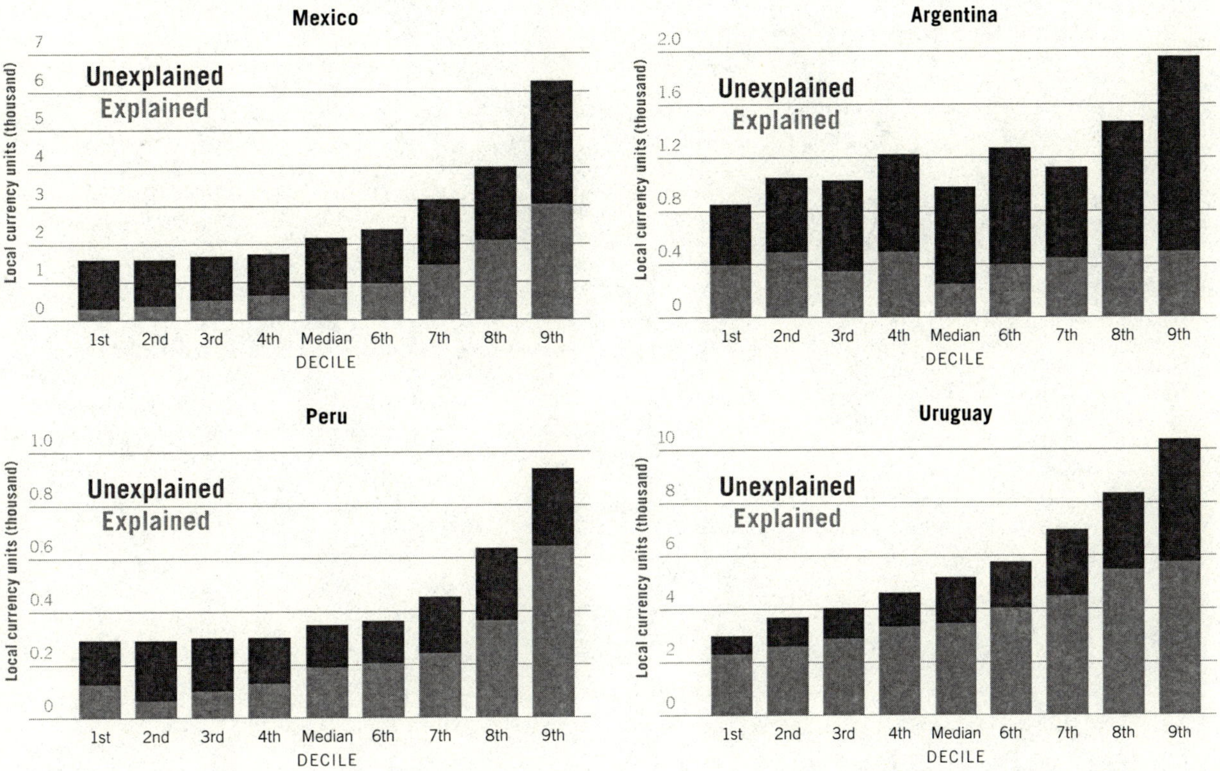

Source: ILO estimates.

Box 8 Informality and labour market segmentation in Argentina

In Argentina, the rate of informal employment increased during the 1990s and then decreased significantly between 2003 and 2011, although it remains high. Taken together, the share in total employment of self-employed and informal paid employees (measured as the share of workers who received wages but are not registered with social security) declined from a peak of more than 60 per cent in the early 2000s to slightly below 50 per cent in 2011. Among paid employees, the rate of non-registered employment dropped from 49.1 per cent in 2003 to 34.5 per cent in 2011. The rate of informal employment among domestic workers (a sector that accounts for 10 per cent of all paid employees, mostly women) climbed from 89 per cent in 1995 to 96.5 per cent in 2003, and then dropped to 84 per cent in 2011.[1] This decline in informality took place in the context of a different macroeconomic policy regime from that of the 1990s, and was achieved in part through a series of policies designed to facilitate formalization and a reversal of earlier policies that had sought to increase labour market flexibility.

In Argentina, results of a statistical analysis which controls for the characteristics of workers show that there was a significant and positive gap of 24.2 per cent in 2010–11 in transitions from informal to formal wage employment, and a smaller, though still significant, gap of 16.3 per cent when moving from informal wage employment to formal wage employment in atypical jobs – that is, on fixed-term or involuntary part-time contracts.

[1] This drop in the percentage of non-registered domestic employees is probably due, in part, to the implementation of tax incentives to register this type of worker.

Source: Bertranou, Casanova, Jiménez and Jiménez, 2013.

PART III | Policy responses to address wages and inequality

11 Introduction: The policy challenge

As noted in the introduction to Part I, debates about wage policy have shifted in recent years and many governments have undertaken new or more ambitious policies to address problems of low wages and wage inequality. This has occurred in some emerging and developing economies as a key component of overall strategies to reduce poverty and inequality. In some developed economies, concerns over deficits in aggregate demand arising from insufficient household consumption have also focused more attention on wages. Many commentators have pointed to the decline or stagnation of wages in most of the Eurozone as increasing the risk of deflation (Wolf, 2014b; OECD, 2014b). Such macroeconomic concerns about aggregate demand and price stability have added to the intensity of the debate over wages. In addition, renewed attention to the problem of increasing inequality in many countries has produced evidence that high inequality slows or interrupts medium- and long-term growth. In an era of slower than trend growth across the world, this has only intensified the search for the factors that contribute to inequality and for suitable policy responses.

In this context, this report has presented the recent evolution of wages across countries and examined the link between wages and inequality. The report has also shown that much of the recent increase in inequality in many countries is driven by changes in wages and wage inequality. The report also highlighted the important role of paid employment in the distribution of incomes. Identifying the factors contributing to rising inequality provides an essential foundation for considering appropriate policy responses.

The report has examined the factor that has traditionally been cited as the most fundamental explanation for the evolution of wages – productivity – and found that in developed economies productivity growth has outstripped wage growth over recent decades and that for the group as a whole, the gap has been widening after a brief pause during the depth of the financial crisis. It is more difficult to identify this relationship over time for emerging and developing economies due to insufficient availability of data, but the report finds that the share of GDP going to labour, which also reflects the link between the growth of wages and labour productivity, has declined over the last decade in China and Mexico, and increased in the Russian Federation.

Another key factor traditionally cited to explain the evolution of wages is returns to education. If higher skills are in greater demand than their supply, for example due to increased use of technological innovations, wages will rise more for the highly skilled, leading to increasing wage inequality. Research in some developed economies has shown that wage premia for graduates have risen since the 1980s – and remained constant in more recent years – despite an expansion in the supply of graduates with tertiary education (Machin, 2009). However, wages have particularly increased for those at the very top of the income distribution, which cannot be linked robustly to education. In emerging and developing countries, the link between education and wages is mixed and in some countries appears to have reversed as larger shares of the population gain higher education.

Other factors explaining the evolution of wages and wage inequality, including globalization and pressure from financial markets for high returns on capital, have been examined in other studies (see for example OECD, 2011; ILO, 2008b; ILO, 2012a). These factors may also have affected the functioning of labour market institutions for redistribution, such as collective bargaining.

The report also looked at factors affecting the wage distribution for certain groups, including women, migrant workers and workers in the informal economy, to provide additional insights into the drivers of recent wage trends and wage inequality.

Having contributed to an understanding of the different factors affecting income and wage inequality, the report now turns to a discussion of appropriate policy responses. As already noted, inequality can arise and be addressed either through policies that affect labour market distribution directly (primary distribution) or through fiscal policies that redistribute through taxation and transfers (secondary distribution). As noted in section 6.2, fiscal redistribution policies in developed economies reduce income inequality by about one-quarter to one-third on average, although the amount of redistribution achieved through those policies appears to have declined in recent years (OECD, 2011). In emerging and developing economies, where tax revenues and social transfers are lower and indirect taxes dominate, fiscal policies tend to play a smaller role in redistribution, although that has increased in countries where governments have pursued aggressive anti-poverty and anti-inequality strategies. Across all countries where the labour share is declining, and in light of increased mobility of capital, there appear to be structural constraints on the degree of redistribution that can be accomplished through fiscal policies. This suggests that inequality that arises within the distribution mechanisms of labour markets must also be addressed through policies that reform those mechanisms to achieve desired reductions in inequality. With less inequality in the labour market, there is less of a need for redistribution through fiscal measures (Berg, forthcoming).

We examine each of these sets of policies in the next sections.

12 Labour market policies to address wages and inequality (primary distribution)

12.1 The role of policies to affect wages and wage distribution directly

Minimum wage policies back in the spotlight

Minimum wages can play an important role in reducing inequality and in supporting the wages of low-paid workers. Recent research supports greater space for utilizing minimum wages, in that new studies or meta-analyses of earlier studies show minimum wages either have no negative effects on employment levels or have very small effects that can be either positive or negative (Betcherman, 2014; Belman and Wolfson, 2014). This is also the finding from meta-analyses carried out for the United States and the United Kingdom (see in particular Doucouliagos and Stanley, 2009, for the United States; Leonard, Stanley and Doucouliagos, 2013, for the United Kingdom).

Fewer studies and detailed meta-analyses exist for emerging and developing economies (Nataraj, Perez-Arce, Srinivasan and Kumar, 2012). However, recent studies have shown that minimum wages – sometimes combined with strengthened collective bargaining – have contributed to reducing inequality in various Latin American countries (see e.g. Keifman and Maurizio, 2012), as well as in other emerging and developing economies. In the Russian Federation, for example, it has been estimated that the reactivation of minimum wage policy explains much of the observed upgrade in wages at the lower end of the wage distribution between 2005 and 2009, particularly for women (Lukyanova, 2011). In Turkey, the introduction of a mandatory minimum wage in 2004 was also a key factor explaining the wage growth at the low end of the wage distribution, which reduced wage inequality and also reduced excessive working hours (Bakis and Polat, 2013; Gönenç and Rawdanowicz, 2010). To have the most positive effects, minimum wages must be well designed and set in a way that balances the needs of workers and their families with economic factors. This principle is reflected in the texts of the ILO Minimum Wage Convention, 1970 (No. 131), and the associated Minimum Wage Fixing Recommendation, 1970 (No. 135), which reflect agreement by governments, employers' organizations and workers' organizations on the essential principles for minimum wage setting and which have been widely utilized, as well as in the recent tripartite discussion at the International Labour Conference (ILO, 2014d).[43]

The role of collective bargaining with respect to wages and wage inequality

Collective bargaining has long been recognized as a key instrument for addressing inequality in general and wage inequality in particular. The ILO's Right to Organise and Collective Bargaining Convention, 1949 (No. 98), has served as a useful guide to governments, employers' organizations and workers' organizations in designing, developing and utilizing collective bargaining for 65 years.

In practice, countries where a large proportion of workers are covered by collective agreements tend to have lower wage inequality (Visser and Checchi, 2009;

Hayter, forthcoming). This is because collective agreements lift wage floors and compress wage distributions, reflecting the fact that union members tend to be motivated both by relative earnings and normative concerns about inequality (Checchi, Visser and van de Werfhorst, 2010). At the same time, the extent to which unionization and collective bargaining affect the wage distribution also depends on whether the collective bargaining system is narrow (where collective bargaining takes place at the company or workplace level) or more inclusive and encompassing (where collective bargaining takes place at the national, industry and/or branch level in multi-employer settings with coordination across levels) (Visser and Checchi, 2009; Hayter, forthcoming). In countries with relatively narrow systems, such as the United States, coverage by collective agreements tends to be lower and top–bottom wage differentials (D9/D1) higher. In more inclusive and encompassing systems, collective agreements tend to cover a larger proportion of workers and top–bottom wage differentials (D9/D1) tend to be lower. Governments may also take policy measures to extend the application of collective agreements to non-signatories, thus reinforcing the equity-enhancing effects of collective bargaining. The extent to which collective bargaining can compress overall wage inequality depends on the position of unionized workers in the pay distribution, the outcome of bargaining for different types of workers, and the degree to which collective bargaining is centralized and coordinated (Bryson, 2007).

Minimum wage policies and collective bargaining should be seen as complements, not alternatives

Institutions interact, and the relationship between statutory minimum wage policies and collective bargaining is perhaps of particular importance. In some countries, relatively high minimum wages can be attributed in part to underdeveloped collective bargaining systems (Lee and McCann, 2014). In such instances, strengthening collective bargaining in addition to effective use of statutory minimum wages is needed to address inequalities. Where collective bargaining is strong and most workers are covered by collective agreements, there has been a perception that there is less need for statutory minimum wages. Yet recent experience in a number of countries with strong collective bargaining systems, such as Germany, indicates that changing economic structures and practices can weaken the impact of collective bargaining systems at low pay levels or in new sectors. In such cases, both appropriate statutory minimum wage policy and robust collective bargaining are needed.

Promoting equal pay across subgroups

As seen in section 10, a significant source of wage inequality can be found in exclusion or discrimination against some categories of workers, including women and migrant workers.

To reduce wage gaps and ensure equal pay across all groups, national legislation must provide for the right to equal remuneration for work of equal value[44] and effective access to justice to claim this right. Labour market institutions and wage policies will only truly be effective in reducing inequality if they are inclusive and cover workers from groups that are vulnerable, disadvantaged and/or subject to discrimination. This requires that the labour market institutions and wage policies do not themselves directly or indirectly discriminate against vulnerable groups of workers (e.g. by setting lower wage levels in sectors or occupations predominantly held by women or excluding migrants from coverage of minimum wage laws). Extending minimum wages and collective agreements to low-paid workers will not eliminate all forms of discrimination. But given the over-representation of women, migrants and other vulnerable groups in low-paying jobs, minimum wage setting and collective bargaining coverage can make a significant contribution to social justice and more inclusive growth.

Overcoming unequal pay across groups requires sustained effort at various levels and through a wide range of policy approaches. Equal pay between men and women needs to be promoted through strong policies to promote gender equality, including combating gender-based stereotypes about women's roles and aspirations, strengthening policies on maternity and paternity as well as parental leave, and advocacy for better sharing of family responsibilities. Equal pay at the enterprise level also requires job evaluation methods free from gender bias.

Equal pay between migrant and national workers can be improved by promoting wider adoption of fair and effective labour migration policies that ensure greater coherence across employment, education/training and development policies at national, regional and global levels. Creating decent work opportunities in countries of origin is also essential to make migration a choice rather than a necessity.

To be effective, policies targeting vulnerable workers must be implemented. This can pose particular challenges in the informal economy and in rural areas, where labour market institutions such as labour inspectorates or collective bargaining are weak.[45] The pay gap between workers in the informal and formal economies can be reduced by laws, policies and practices which facilitate transitions from the informal to formal economy. The ILO is currently undertaking a standard-setting process with a view to creating a Recommendation on facilitating transition from the informal to the formal economy, and will thus provide policy guidance in this domain.

Finally, there continues to be a need for improved analysis to understand the pay gaps in different countries and to monitor their evolution, including a better understanding of the reasons underlying explained and unexplained components of pay gaps.

Promoting job creation

Job creation is a priority in all countries, and this report has shown that access to, and loss of, paid employment are a key determinant of income inequality. In developed economies, job losses that disproportionately affect low-income workers contributed to increasing inequality. In emerging and developing economies, the creation of paid employment for those at the bottom helped reduce inequality in a number of cases. These findings confirm that the pursuit of full-employment policies is an important tool in reducing inequality (see also Berg, forthcoming).

In addition to hurting persons looking for paid employment, unemployment or excess labour supply can also weaken the wage growth of those who are in paid employment. A comprehensive and integrated approach to achieving the goal of full employment is embedded in the ILO Employment Policy Convention, 1964 (No. 122), as well as the Global Employment Agenda (2003) and the conclusions of the recurrent item discussion on employment by the International Labour Conference (2010). The promotion of sustainable enterprises can be key in this regard. This involves creating an enabling environment for enterprises to start and grow, as well as encouraging innovation and enhancing productivity. The resulting benefits can be shared equitably both within enterprises and in society more broadly.

12.2 The role of policies to affect wages and wage distribution indirectly

Growing wage inequality in developed economies has been attributed to an increase in the relative demand for skilled labour due to a combination of technological change biased in favour of skilled workers (skill-biased technical change) and the growing exposure of unskilled workers to international competition (Atkinson, 2007), although, as noted above, wage stagnation among workers with higher education in recent years suggests that other factors may at times be more important. In emerging and developing economies, there has been a dynamic evolution of returns to education. In the case of Latin America, the decline in wage inequality from the mid-1990s, after an increase in the early 1990s, is often attributed to the expansion in education and the associated decline in returns to education (López-Calva and Lustig, 2010; Keifman and Maurizio, 2012; Azevedo, Davalos, Diaz-Bonilla, Atuesta and Castañeda, 2013; Gasparini and Lustig, 2011; Birdsall, Lustig and McLeod, 2011; Gasparini, Cruces and Tornarolli, 2009; Cornia, 2012). In urban China, the rate of returns to education began to climb in the early 1990s and continued to increase sharply thereafter (Naughton, 2007), leading to higher average wages, but also to a rise in inequality.

While other factors have influenced these outcomes, sustained attention to equal access to education, policies to increase the skills of the labour force, particularly those at the bottom of the distribution, and better analysis to improve matching of labour skill demand and supply are appropriate in all countries.

The issue of appropriate skills is particularly relevant for current jobseekers. Indeed, an important source of income inequality is the high incidence of unemployment in many economies and the resulting downward pressure on wages for most categories of workers. It is important to ensure that unemployed workers remain attached to the labour market and retain or upgrade their skills to reduce the risk that their earnings potential erodes, thereby exacerbating inequality. In this regard, labour market analysis of skill needs and labour market policies, including training programmes and job-matching services, are essential to improving re-employment prospects and mitigating potential sources of future inequality.

In addition to education, many other factors have been highlighted as contributing to wage inequality. Some of these arise in the context of labour markets, such as the "casualization" of part of the labour force through involuntary temporary or involuntary part-time employment.[46] Policies to address these sources of inequality include regulatory reforms to avoid lower costs associated with non-standard workers, such as when part-time workers fall under the threshold of social security benefits or if fixed-term workers are exempt from severance pay (Gleason, 2006). Others arise at the margin of labour markets, for example changing norms with regard to the salaries and bonuses of CEOs. While these may be amenable to policy intervention, they will entail policies outside the labour market.

13 Fiscal policies to address wages and inequality (secondary distribution)

As noted above, fiscal policies are also employed by governments to address their income distribution objectives. These tools tend to be used more in developed economies than in emerging and developing economies, although there may be some convergence under way; the amount of redistribution achieved through those policies in developed economies appears to have declined in recent years while a number of governments in emerging and developing economies have stepped up their use of transfers to address equity objectives and poverty reduction.

We now turn to the specific elements of the fiscal tools for redistribution: taxes and transfers.

13.1 The role of taxes

We may be observing increasing structural constraints on the degree of redistribution that can be accomplished through taxation policies in developed economies. In countries where the labour income share is declining, revenue mobilization, through taxes on labour income, will also decline unless (1) the labour share is increased or (2) tax rates on labour income are increased. In many developed economies, taxation systems have become less progressive over recent years, and this suggests that higher rates of taxation on wage income at the low and middle ranges of the distribution would increase total inequality and be perceived as highly unfair in light of the increased labour market inequality (OECD, 2012b). This argues for addressing the declining labour share more directly through the labour market policies and mechanisms discussed above.

In most emerging and developing economies, there appears to be space for improved collection of taxes on labour income through a variety of measures. Depending on country circumstances, these may include efforts to formalize informal enterprises and workers to broaden the tax base (as well as to bring them into the realm of contributory social protection schemes, discussed below); improving the progressivity of tax schedules so that the highest earners pay a larger share of the overall tax burden; and improved tax collection.

In both developed economies and emerging and developing economies, there has been some successful experience with targeted tax reduction, elimination or even positive tax credits to low-income households as ways to increase their overall income and also to provide positive incentives for work. Policies such as earned income tax credits for low-wage workers have increased the net income from work for their households (Immervoll and Pearson, 2009; Immervoll, 2009). While these mechanisms operate through the tax code, they are more correctly understood as targeted transfers.

Progressive personal income taxes and directed tax efforts toward greater equality play an important role, but in practice most of the reduction in inequality through fiscal policy is achieved on the expenditure side through transfers, discussed below (IMF, 2014b; OECD, 2011).

The ability of governments to shift taxation to capital (as a source of revenues for redistribution and a means to increase the progressivity of overall taxation systems) is also constrained, in this case by the increased mobility of capital in the context of globalization and reduction of barriers to cross-border capital mobility. Taxation of capital has also been evaded by firms that use tax avoidance and cross-border profit-shifting strategies to minimize payment of taxes to any government. There has been an increasing recognition by governments and experts in recent years that these avoidance and evasion strategies must be addressed through cross-border policy coordination. The G20 in particular, supported by the OECD, has made a priority of addressing these problems, beginning with a campaign for automatic exchange of tax information (G20, 2014b). These efforts have been extended to countries outside the G20 and OECD membership with some success.

13.2 The role of social protection and its relationship to labour market policies

The other policy instrument for post-market or secondary redistribution is the use of transfers, which arise in many different forms. These include direct payments to low-income households, such as: cash transfer systems; the creation of public employment opportunities for low-income workers or households, such as the rural employment guarantee scheme in India; direct or subsidized provision by governments to low-income households of food or production inputs, such as seeds; pensions; publicly provided or financed health care; and public education, among others. Collectively, these efforts are referred to as social protection or social protection systems. The ILO and others have demonstrated the role of social protection systems in reducing inequality and contributing to more inclusive growth.[47]

The appropriate design and mix of social protection measures will vary from country to country, depending on the overall level of income and economic development, the stage of structural transformation of the economy from agriculture to manufacturing and services, the distribution of the poor between rural and urban areas, the existence of vulnerable or excluded groups and other factors.[48] However, some general lessons can be drawn from the patterns of wage and total income distribution presented in sections 7–10 of Part II.

14 Conclusion: Combined policy actions can address inequality, promote employment and support aggregate demand

As seen in figures 29 and 32, wages constitute the largest single source of income for households in developed economies and emerging and developing economies, with only a few exceptions. At the same time, wages make only a small contribution to household income for the lowest income groups (as seen in figures 30, 31, 33 and 34). In developed economies, this applies mainly to the bottom 10 per cent of households, where social protection transfers are more important sources of income for these households in the United States and northern Europe. This suggests that policies to help individuals in these households to move into employment (through measures such as active support for job search, training, childcare expenses, transportation, etc.) combined with measures to make the work they find more remunerative (through minimum wages, tax credits, etc.) will help these households to gradually move up the income scale. In some developed economies, for example in many southern European countries, self-employment makes up a larger source of income for the bottom decile of households. Some of the same policies mentioned above may be appropriate to help individuals in these households move into paid employment, but in addition, other policies, such as access to financial and business services, may be needed as well.

In some emerging and developing economies, wages also represent a relatively minor share of income for households in the bottom decile, but in some countries in this group, this pertains throughout the bottom third or more of the income distribution. With fewer social transfers, income from self-employment and other income sources (such as remittances) are more important factors. This suggests that while improving wages will be a part of the policy response to addressing inequality for these households, other measures to support their incomes will also be needed. Here successes have been achieved through direct employment programmes (as in India and South Africa) and conditional or unconditional cash transfers (as in Brazil and Mexico, among many others). Gradual formalization of informal self-employment, through measures such as organization of cooperatives, entrepreneurship training and tailored business development services to microenterprises, can also benefit such households. It is also important to recognize that the most effective route out of poverty for these households is finding a job, and if that job pays at least the minimum wage the household may move up to the next decile of the income distribution.

All of these policies can be made more effective by conscious development of strategies to address inequality and poverty that include coherence and complementarity between social protection, wage and taxation policies. Gradually, social protection can lift households above subsistence level and allow them to invest in their own productive potential, including through education of children, acquisition of skills by adults and productivity-enhancing investment in agriculture or other self-employment activities. Macroeconomic policies that favour expansion of job creation as well as price stability can help create more employment opportunities for individuals in these and other households in the lower half of the income distribution and therefore allow them to benefit more from pro-equity wage policies. Coherent policies can thus foster a virtuous cycle, whereby higher wages and incomes lead to more consumption and therefore more aggregate demand and investment. The same virtuous cycle will also produce higher tax payments and government revenues, which allow for further policies to increase income equity and growth without added debt, for example through additional investment in infrastructure that benefits all segments of society, improvement in the quality of education and health care for lower-income households, and so on.

Coherent strategies are also needed at international level, to coordinate macroeconomic policies as well as to jointly agree on approaches to wages, employment and social protection policies to boost household income and consumption. If individual countries try to maximize their growth through actions to increase exports such as cutting wages, it may work for one country or several small countries, but at the global level it will reduce aggregate demand and therefore constitute a beggar-thy-neighbour approach rather than a general welfare-enhancing approach. If many countries were to follow this approach, the consequences could be a serious contraction of output and trade.

Appendix I

Global wage trends: Methodological issues

The methodology to estimate global and regional wage trends was developed by the ILO's Inclusive Labour Markets, Labour Relations and Working Conditions Branch (INWORK)[49] for the previous *Global Wage Reports* in collaboration with the Department of Statistics, following proposals formulated by an ILO consultant and three peer reviews made by four independent experts.[50] This appendix describes the methodology adopted as a result of this process.

Concepts and definitions

- According to the international classification of status in employment (ICSE-93), "employees" are workers who hold "paid employment jobs", i.e. jobs in which the basic remuneration is not directly dependent on the revenue of the employer. Employees include regular employees, workers in short-term employment, casual workers, outworkers, seasonal workers and other categories of workers holding paid employment jobs (ILO, 1993b).
- The word "wage" refers to total gross remuneration including regular bonuses received by employees during a specified period of time for time worked as well as time not worked, such as paid annual leave and paid sick leave. Essentially, it corresponds to the concept of "total cash remuneration", which is the major component of income related to paid employment (ILO, 1998). It excludes employers' social security contributions.
- Wages, in the present context, refer to real average monthly wages of employees. Wherever possible, we collected data that refer to all employees (rather than to a subset, such as employees in manufacturing or full-time employees).[51] To adjust for the influence of price changes over different time periods, wages are measured in real terms, i.e. the nominal wage data are adjusted for consumer price inflation in the respective country.[52] Real wage growth refers to the year-on-year change in average monthly real wages of all employees.

Census approach

The methodology used for the global and regional estimates is a census method with non-response. In the census approach, the objective is to find wage data for all countries and to develop an explicit treatment in the case of total non-response (see "Treatment of total non-response", below). We have tried to collect wage data for a total of 178 countries and territories, grouped into six separate regions.[53]

Table A1 Regional groups

Regional group	Countries and territories
Developed economies	Australia, Austria, Belgium, Bulgaria, Canada, Cyprus, Czech Republic, Denmark, Estonia, Finland, France, Germany, Greece, Hungary, Iceland, Ireland, Israel, Italy, Japan, Latvia, Lithuania, Luxembourg, Malta, Netherlands, New Zealand, Norway, Poland, Portugal, Romania, Slovakia, Slovenia, Spain, Sweden, Switzerland, United Kingdom, United States
Eastern Europe and Central Asia	Albania, Armenia, Azerbaijan, Belarus, Bosnia and Herzegovina, Croatia, Georgia, Kazakhstan, Kyrgyzstan, Republic of Moldova, Montenegro, Russian Federation, Serbia, Tajikistan, The Former Yugoslav Republic of Macedonia, Turkey, Turkmenistan, Ukraine, Uzbekistan
Asia and the Pacific	Afghanistan, Bangladesh, Bhutan, Brunei, Cambodia, China, Fiji, Hong Kong (China), India, Indonesia, Islamic Republic of Iran, Democratic People's Republic of Korea, Republic of Korea, Lao People's Democratic Republic, Macau (China), Malaysia, Republic of Maldives, Mongolia, Myanmar, Nepal, Pakistan, Papua New Guinea, Philippines, Singapore, Solomon Islands, Sri Lanka, Taiwan (China), Thailand, Timor-Leste, Viet Nam
Latin America and the Caribbean	Argentina,* Bahamas, Barbados, Belize, Plurinational State of Bolivia, Brazil, Chile, Colombia, Costa Rica, Cuba, Dominican Republic, Ecuador, El Salvador, Guadeloupe, Guatemala, Guyana, Haiti, Honduras, Jamaica, Martinique, Mexico, Nicaragua, Panama, Paraguay, Peru, Puerto Rico, Suriname, Trinidad and Tobago, Uruguay, Bolivarian Republic of Venezuela
Middle East	Bahrain, Iraq, Jordan, Kuwait, Lebanon, Oman, Qatar, Saudi Arabia, Syrian Arab Republic, United Arab Emirates, West Bank and Gaza, Yemen
Africa	Algeria, Angola, Benin, Botswana, Burkina Faso, Burundi, Cameroon, Cabo Verde, Central African Republic, Chad, Comoros, Congo, Côte d'Ivoire, Democratic Republic of the Congo, Egypt, Equatorial Guinea, Eritrea, Ethiopia, Gabon, Gambia, Ghana, Guinea, Guinea-Bissau, Kenya, Lesotho, Liberia, Libya, Madagascar, Malawi, Mali, Mauritania, Mauritius, Morocco, Mozambique, Namibia, Niger, Nigeria, Réunion, Rwanda, Senegal, Sierra Leone, Somalia, South Africa, Sudan, Swaziland, United Republic of Tanzania, Togo, Tunisia, Uganda, Zambia, Zimbabwe

* Argentina identified some inconsistencies in its wage series for some years and has been excluded.

Table A2 Coverage of the ILO Global Wage Database, 2013 (%)

Regional group	Country coverage	Employee coverage	Approximate coverage of total wage bill
Africa	45.1	65.7	81.0
Asia	73.3	98.4	99.5
Developed economies	100.0	100.0	100.0
Eastern Europe and Central Asia	100.0	100.0	100.0
Latin America and the Caribbean	72.4	94.4	95.5
Middle East	75.0	73.1	87.3
World	**73.4**	**95.8**	**98.6**

Note: Country coverage refers to the number of countries for which we found wage data as a percentage of all the countries in the region; employee coverage refers to the number of employees in countries with data available as a percentage of all employees in the region (as of 2013). The approximate coverage of total wages is estimated based on the assumption that wage levels vary across countries in line with labour productivity (i.e. GDP per person employed, as of 2013), expressed in 2005 PPP$.

To enable easier comparison to regional employment trends, our regional groupings are compatible with those used in the ILO's Global Employment Trends Model (GET Model) (see table A1). However, we have collapsed several GET regions into a single region for Asia (which includes the GET regions East Asia, South-East Asia and the Pacific, and South Asia) and for Africa (which comprises North Africa and sub-Saharan Africa).

Overall, we found wage data from 130 countries and territories, with regional coverage indicated in table A2. We have data from developed economies and all countries in Eastern Europe and Central Asia. Although repeated attempts were made to obtain wage figures from national statistical offices and/or international repositories, in some instances wage data were not available. The coverage for the remaining regions ranges from 45.1 per cent (Africa) to 75.0 per cent (Middle East). However, since the database includes wage data for the largest and more prosperous countries, the coverage in terms of employees and the total wage bill is higher than the simple count of countries would suggest. In total, our database contains information for 95.8 per cent of the world's employees, who among them account for approximately 98.6 per cent of the world's wage bill.

Treatment of item non-response

In some countries for which we found data, the statistical series were incomplete, in the sense that data for some years were missing. Table A3 provides coverage information for each year from 2006 to 2013. As expected, the coverage of the database becomes lower for the most recent years since some statistical offices are still processing these data. Consequently, for 2013 we have real observations for only about 90.9 per cent of the world's total wages, as compared to 96.8 per cent in 2011.

While the coverage in the most recent year is good in the developed economies and in Eastern Europe and Central Asia, in other regions, such as the Middle East and Africa, it is less so. For this reason, regional growth rates are flagged

Table A3 Coverage of the ILO Global Wage Database, 2006–13 (%)

Regional group	2006	2007	2008	2009	2010	2011	2012	2013
Africa	68.0*	66.9*	67.2*	68.0*	67.8*	79.7	77.7	42.7*
Asia	99.5	99.5	99.5	99.4	99.2	94.0	94.4	86.4
Developed economies	100.0	100.0	100.0	100.0	100.0	100.0	100.0	96.3
Eastern Europe and Central Asia	98.3	98.9	98.8	98.6	98.5	100.0	100.0	97.7
Latin America and the Caribbean	94.4	94.4	94.1	94.0	92.9	95.2	95.2	90.4
Middle East	87.5	87.8	88.0	67.4*	(27.4)	64.9*	57.5*	52.0*
World	**98.3**	**98.3**	**98.2**	**97.5**	**96.0**	**96.8**	**96.5**	**90.9**

* Growth rates published as "tentative estimates" (based on coverage *c.* 40–74%).
() Growth rates published but likely to change (based on coverage of less than 40%).
Note: See text for estimation of coverage. A country is counted as covered only when a real observation is available, either from a primary or secondary source.

as "tentative estimates" when the underlying coverage of our database is between 40 and 74 per cent, to draw attention to fact that they might be revised once additional data become available.

To address this kind of item non-response (i.e. gaps in countries for which we have data) a "model-based framework" is used to predict missing values.[54] This is necessary in order to hold the set of responding countries constant over time and thus avoid the undesired effects associated with an unstable sample. Depending on the nature of the missing data points, several complementary approaches were used; these are described in detail in Technical Appendix I of the 2010/11 edition of the *Global Wage Report*.

Treatment of total non-response

Response weights

To adjust for total non-response (when no time-series wage data are available for a given country), a "design-based framework" was used in which non-response was considered as a sampling problem. Because non-responding countries may have wage characteristics that differ from those of responding countries, non-response may introduce a bias into the final estimates. A standard approach to reduce the adverse effect of non-response is to calculate the propensity of response of different countries and then weight the data from responding countries by the inverse of their response propensity.[55] This implies that no imputations are made for non-responding countries.

In this framework, each country responds with a probability φ_j and it is assumed that countries respond independently of each other (Poisson sampling design). With the probabilities of response, φ_j, it is then possible to estimate the total, Y, of any variable y_j:

$$Y = \sum_{j \in U} y_j \tag{1}$$

by the estimator

$$\hat{Y} = \sum_{j \in R} \frac{y_j}{\varphi_j} \tag{2}$$

where U is the population and R is the set of respondents. This estimator is unbiased if the assumptions are true (see Tillé, 2001). In our case, U is the universe of all countries and territories listed in table A1 and R is those "responding" countries for which we could find time-series wage data.

The difficulty, however, is that the response propensity of country j, φ_j, is generally not known and must itself be estimated. Many methods are available in the literature to estimate the response propensity (see e.g. Tillé, 2001). In our case, the response propensity was estimated by relating the response or non-response of a given country to its number of employees and its labour productivity (or GDP per person employed in 2005 PPP$). This is based on the observation that wage statistics are more readily available for richer and larger countries than for poorer and smaller countries. The number of employees and labour productivity are used since these variables are also used for calibration and size weighting (see below).[56]

For this purpose, we estimated a logistic regression with fixed effects as follows:

$$prob(response) = \Lambda(\alpha_h + \beta_1 x_{j2006} + \beta_2 n_{j2006}) \tag{3}$$

where x_{j2006} is ln(GDP per person employed in 2005 PPP$) of country j in the year 2006, n_{j2006} is ln(number of employees) in 2006, and Λ denotes the logistic cumulative distribution function (CDF).[57] The year 2006 is chosen because it is the midpoint between 1999 and 2013. The fixed effects, α_h, are dummies for each of the regions with incomplete data (Asia and the Pacific, Latin America and the Caribbean, the Middle East, Africa), while the two remaining regions with complete data form the omitted benchmark category. The logistic regression had a universe of N = 177 cases and produced a pseudo $R^2 = 0.230$. The estimated parameters were then used to calculate the propensity of response of country j, φ_j.

The response weight for country j, ϕ_j, is then given by the inverse of a country's response propensity:

$$\phi_j = \frac{1}{\varphi_j} \tag{4}$$

Calibration factors

The final adjustment process, generally called calibration (Särndal and Deville, 1992), is undertaken to ensure consistency of the estimate with known aggregates. This procedure ensures appropriate representation of the different regions in the final global estimate. In the present context, a single variable "number of employees", n, in a given year t was considered for calibration. In this simple case, the calibration factors, γ_{it}, are given by

$$\gamma_{jt} = \frac{n_{ht}}{\hat{n}_{ht}}, j \in h \tag{5}$$

where h represents the region to which country j belongs, n_{ht} is the known number of employees in that region in year t, and $\hat{n}_{ht}$ is an estimate of total number of employees in the region and the same year, obtained as a sum product of the uncalibrated weights and the employment data from the responding countries within each region.[58]

The resulting calibration factors for the year 2010 were 1.00 (developed economies; Eastern Europe and Central Asia), 1.01 (Asia and the Pacific), 0.972 (Latin America and the Caribbean), 1.03 (Africa) and 1.14 (Middle East). Since all calibration factors are either equal to or very close to 1, these results show that estimates $\hat{n}_{ht}$ were already very close to the known number of employees, n_{ht} in each region. Note the calibration process was repeated for each year so that the weight of each region in the global estimate changes over time in proportion to its approximate share in the global wage bill.

Calibrated response weights

The calibrated response weights, ϕ'_{jt}, are then obtained by multiplying the initial response weight with the calibration factor:

$$\phi'_{jt} = \phi_j \times \gamma_{it} \tag{6}$$

The regional estimate of the number of employees based on the calibrated response weights is equal to the known total number of employees in that region and a given year. Thus, the calibrated response weights adjust for differences in non-response between regions. The calibrated response weights are equal to 1 in the regions where wage data were available for all countries (developed economies; Eastern Europe and Central Asia). They are larger than 1 for small countries and countries with lower labour productivity since these are under-represented among responding countries.

Estimating global and regional trends

One intuitive way to think of a global (or regional) wage trend is in terms of the evolution of the world's (or a region's) average wage. This would be in line with the concept used for other well-known estimates, such as regional GDP per capita growth (published by the World Bank) or the change in labour productivity (or GDP per person employed).

The global average wage, $\bar{y}_t$, at the point in time t can be obtained by dividing the sum of the national wage bills by the global number of employees:

$$\bar{y}_t = \frac{\sum_j n_{jt} \times \bar{y}_{jt}}{\sum_j n_{jt}} \tag{7}$$

where n_{jt} is the number of employees in country j and $\bar{y}_{jt}$ is the corresponding average wage of employees in country j, both at time t.

The same can be repeated for the preceding time period t+1 to obtain $\bar{y}^*_{t+1}$, using the deflated wages $\bar{y}^*_{jt+1}$ and the number of employees n_{t+1}. It is then straightforward to calculate the growth rate of the global average wage, r.

However, while this is a conceptually appealing way to estimate global wage trends, it involves some difficulties that we cannot at present overcome. In particular, aggregating national wages, as done in equation (7), requires them to be converted into a common currency, such as PPP$. This conversion would make the estimates sensitive to revisions in PPP conversion factors. It would also require that national wage statistics be harmonized to a single concept of wages in order to make the level strictly comparable.[59]

More importantly, the change in the global average wage would also be influenced by composition effects that occur when the share of employees shifts between countries. For instance, if the number of paid employees falls in a country with high wages but expands (or stays constant) in a country of similar size with low wages, this would result in a fall of the global average wage (when wage levels stay constant in all countries). This effect makes changes in the global average wage difficult to interpret, as one would have to differentiate which part is due to changes in national average wages and which part is due to composition effects.

We therefore gave preference to an alternative specification to calculate global wage trends that maintains the intuitive appeal of the concept presented above but avoids its practical challenges. To ease interpretation, we also want to exclude effects that are due to changes in the composition of the world's employee population. We therefore avoid the danger of producing a statistical artefact of falling global average wages that could be caused by a shift in employment to low-wage countries (even when wages within countries are actually growing).

When the number of employees in each country is held constant, the global wage growth rate can be expressed as a weighted average of the wage growth rates in the individual countries:

$$r_t = \sum_j w_{jt} \times r_{jt} \tag{8}$$

where r_{jt} is wage growth in country j at point in time t and the country weight, w_{jt}, is the share of country j in the global wage bill, as given by:

$$w_{jt} = n_{jt} \times \bar{y}_{jt} / \sum_j n_{jt} \times \bar{y}_{jt} \tag{9}$$

While we have data for the number of employees, n_{jt}, in all countries and relevant points in time from the ILO's Global Employment Trends Model, we cannot estimate equation (9) directly since our wage data are not in a common currency. However, we can again draw on standard economic theory which suggests that average wages vary roughly in line with labour productivity across countries.[60] We can thus estimate $\bar{y}_j$ as a fixed proportion of labour productivity, LP:

$$\hat{\bar{y}}_{jt} = \alpha \times LP_{jt} \tag{10}$$

where α is the average ratio of wages over labour productivity. We can therefore estimate the weight as

$$\hat{w}_{jt} = n_{jt} \times \alpha \times LP_{jt} / \sum_j n_{jt} \times \alpha \times LP_{jt} \tag{11}$$

which is equal to

$$\hat{w}_{jt} = n_{jt} \times LP_{jt} / \sum_j n_{jt} \times LP_{jt} \tag{12}$$

Substituting $\hat{w}_{jt}$ for w_{jt} and introducing the calibrated response weight, ϕ'_j, into equation (8) gives us the final equation used to estimate global wage growth:

$$r_t = \frac{\sum_j \phi'_j \times \hat{w}_{jt} \times r_{jt}}{\sum_j \phi'_j \times \hat{w}_{jt}} \tag{13}$$

and for regional wage growth:

$$r_{ht} = \frac{\sum_j \phi'_j \times \hat{w}_{jt} \times r_{jt}}{\sum_j \phi'_j \times \hat{w}_{jt}}, j \in h \tag{13'}$$

where h is the region of which country j is part. As can be seen from equations (13) and (13'), global and regional wage growth rates are the weighted averages of the national wage trends, where ϕ'_j corrects for differences in response propensities between countries.

Differences in global and regional estimates between editions of the *Global Wage Report*

Since 2010, when the publication of regional and global wage growth estimates using the methodology outlined above began, there have been slight revisions to the historical estimates. While these revisions are relatively minor in some regions, such as the developed economies and Eastern Europe and Central Asia, they are more frequent and sometimes substantial in others. The revisions to regional estimates can be explained by several factors, briefly highlighted here.

1. **Improvements and revisions to surveys which collect wage data.** Improvements and revisions to existing wage data and surveys often occur. These may include a change in the geographical coverage (e.g. from urban to national), a change in sector coverage (e.g. from manufacturing to all sectors), a change in employee coverage (e.g. from full-time employees only to all employees) etc. To the extent these changes influence the growth in wages, they may also influence the regional estimate.

2. **Exclusions.** In Latin America, Argentina has been excluded since the 2012 version of the *Global Wage Report* (ILO, 2012a) because it identified inconsistencies in its wage series.

3. **Availability of new data from non-response and response countries.** Particularly in emerging and developing economies, there is often a lag in the process time for data and/or their public availability. When new or older series are made available, they are incorporated into the regional estimates.

4. **Revision of other data sources used to calculate the estimates.** Over time, revisions to the CPI, total employment, total employees and labour productivity can also influence regional and country estimates.

Appendix II

Definitions, concepts and data issues

Concepts, definitions and measures

As previously mentioned, wages and household income are two separate, but related, concepts. While wages refer to gross remuneration in cash and in kind paid to employees, household income is measured at the household level, and includes all receipts received by the household or by its individual members (see definitions in box A1). Wages are a key source of household income, but they are not the only source of income, and sometimes not even the main source. Figure A1 shows how different income components can be aggregated to produce *total household income*. We see that employment-related income includes both employee income (one component of which is wages) and income from self-employment. In addition, total household income also comprises property income (such as interests, dividends, and rents that arise from the ownership of financial or non-financial assets), income of services for own consumption (such as imputed rents and unpaid domestic services) and current transfers (which include government sponsored social insurance schemes, employers sponsored benefits, social assistance benefits, and transfers from other households or non-profit institutions such as unions). For detailed definitions of each of these concepts, see box A1.

Figure A1 The components of household income

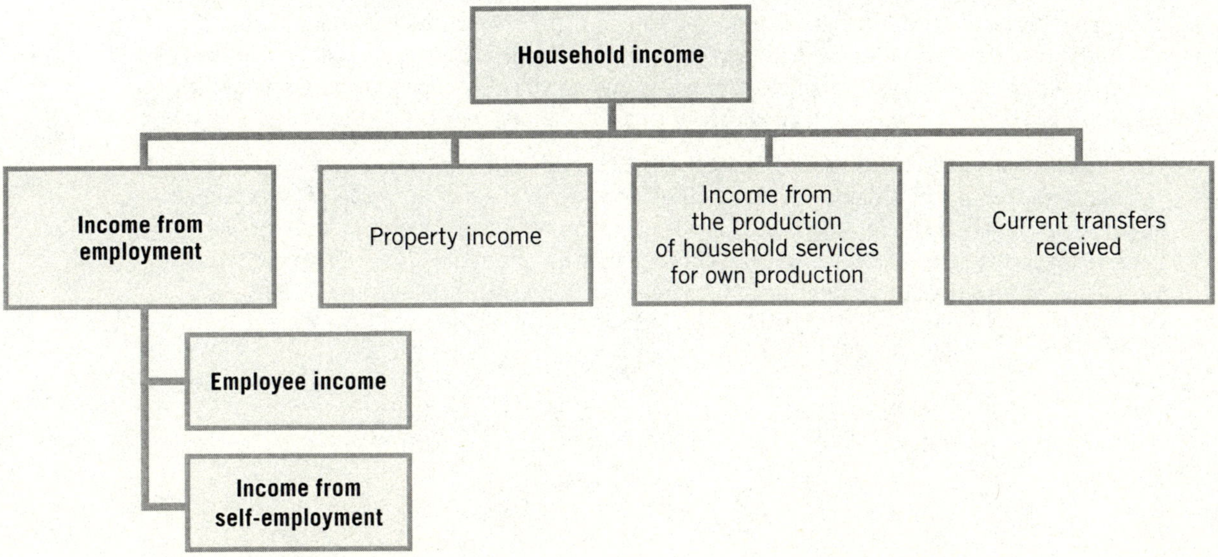

Source: ILO, 2003b.

Box A1 Concepts and definitions

Household income consists of all receipts, whether monetary or in kind (goods and services), that are received by the household or by individual members of the household at annual or more frequent intervals, but excludes windfall gains and other such irregular and typically one-time receipts. Household income receipts are available for current consumption and do not reduce the net worth of the household through a reduction of its cash, the disposal of its other financial or non-financial assets or an increase in its liabilities. Household income may be defined to cover: (i) income from employment (both paid and self-employment); (ii) property income; (iii) income from the production of household services for own consumption; and (iv) current transfers received.

Employee income comprises direct wages and salaries for time worked and work done, cash bonuses and gratuities, commissions and tips, directors' fees, profit-sharing bonuses and other forms of profit-related pay, remuneration for time not worked, and free or subsidized goods and services from an employer. It may include severance and termination pay as well as employers' social insurance contributions. These items should be reported separately, when included. The definition of these terms is consistent with their use in the resolution concerning the measurement of employment-related income adopted by the 16th International Conference of Labour Statisticians (ILO, 1998).

Employee income may be received in cash (monetary) or in kind as goods or services. Those receipts in kind that are outputs of the employer's production process should be included only in so far as they are in line with the recommendations contained in the ILO's Protection of Wages Convention, 1949 (No. 95). Otherwise, they are imposed payments in kind that should be excluded from employee income or valued at zero.

Wages are a component of *employee income* and for the purpose of this report refer to the statistical concept of earnings (for a definition, see box 1 in Part I).

Income from self-employment is income received by individuals, over a given reference period, as a result of their involvement in self-employment jobs as defined in the resolution concerning the International Classification of Status in Employment adopted by the 15th International Conference of Labour Statisticians (ILO, 1993b). In particular, income from self-employment concerns primarily owners of unincorporated enterprises who work in these enterprises. It excludes profits from capital investment of partners who do not work in these enterprises ("sleeping partners"), dividends, and directors' fees paid to owners of incorporated enterprises. Income from self-employment includes the estimated value of goods and services produced for barter as well as goods produced for own consumption, less expenses.

The basis for the measurement of income from self-employment is the concept of mixed income defined by the System of National Accounts. Mixed income consists of the value of gross output less operating costs and after adjustment for depreciation of assets used in production, where these terms are as defined in the resolution concerning the measurement of employment-related income adopted by the 16th International Conference of Labour Statisticians (ILO, 1998).

Source: ILO, 2003b.

Because income is measured at the household level, ranking households from richest to poorest (in terms of household income) requires not only information on total household income, but also information on the size of the household. An annual household income of US$6,500 is not the same for a single-person household as it is for a household with two adults and three children. In order to rank households from richest to poorest, a per capita household income is calculated. Since there are economies of scale when several individuals live together, and because children have lower material needs than adults (in terms of calories, for example), estimating per capita income requires the use of equivalence scales. The method used is explained in box A2.

The fact that household members' economic well-being depends on per capita, rather than total, household income implies that changes in household income inequality depend not only on changes in the level of income per se from different sources but also on demographic factors, such as changes in the population age structure or family living arrangements. So, for example, the trend in OECD countries towards smaller families – with a growing number of single-headed households – tends to increase household income inequality and poverty rates; similarly, the growing percentage of households with retired members creates a larger number of households with relatively smaller incomes.[61] "Assortative mating" (the tendency of high-wage earners to marry other high-wage earners) also increases household income inequality, and seems to have contributed somewhat to widening inequality in OECD-type countries.[62] However, these factors generally operate over the medium to long term, and are in any event beyond the scope of this report.

Other elements that contribute to households' economic well-being, but are beyond the scope of this analysis, include both household wealth (assets minus liabilities) and the extent to which governments provide free or subsidized medical services, education, or other goods and services that also affect people's material well-being. To take this latter element into account, household income would have to be adjusted for the value of these *social transfers in kind* (STIK), but this is a difficult undertaking. Note also that this report decomposes total household income, as opposed to disposable household income, because disposable household income is not frequently available.[63]

Box A2 Measuring per capita household income

Household income can be measured as the sum of incomes from all different sources accruing to a given household over a certain period of time. The link between total household income and living standards depends on the number of persons who must live on this income: a total annual income of, say, US$6,500 does not have the same meaning for a single-person household as it does for a household with two adults and three children. To account for family size, and reflect living standards, we could simply divide total household income by the number of household members. In the hypothetical case illustrated in figure A2, we would divide US$6,500 by five, and obtain a per capita household income of US$1,300.

Figure A2 Illustration of the components of household income

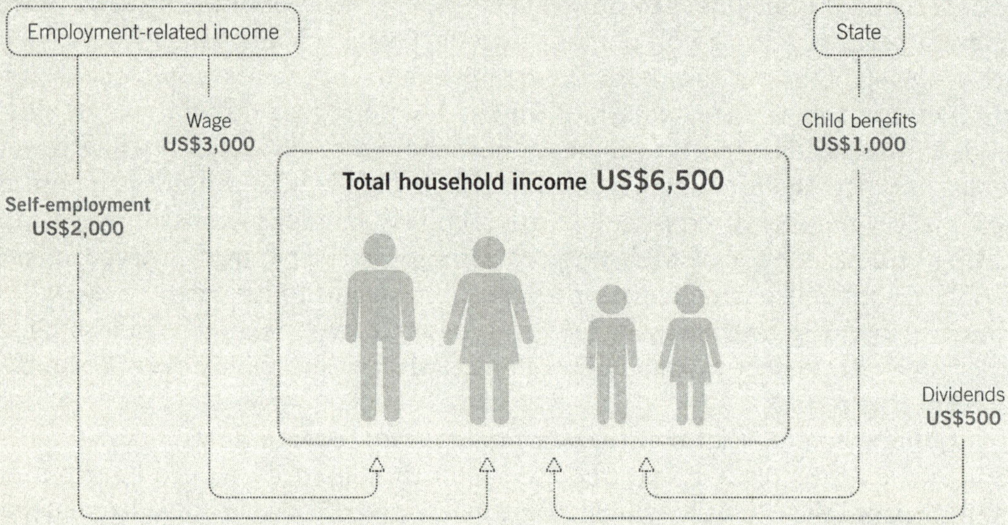

Such a simple method, however, does not take into account the fact that there exist economies of scale when people live together (e.g. only one dwelling instead of two), and that children need fewer calories than adults. To take these further considerations into account, and to obtain an adjusted measure of the "possibility of households to consume", we follow Deaton and Zaidi's formula and calculate per capita household income as: $E=(A+\alpha K)^{\theta}$ where A represents the number of adults, K is the number of dependent children, α represents the spending of a child relative to an adult, and θ captures the economies of scale in a given household (Deaton and Zaidi, 2002). We use the adjustment factors as specified in table A4, and illustrate the use of the formula with our hypothetical example. We see that the effective per capita household income would be set in a range from US$2,493 to US$2,728.

Table A4 Equivalent scale parameters guide

	α	θ	In our example:
Advanced economies	0.75	0.6	PCHHI = $6500 \div (2+0.75\times3)^{0.6}$ = US$ 2728
Middle-income or emerging economies	0.50	0.8	PCHHI = $6500 \div (2+0.50\times3)^{0.75}$ = US$ 2540
Low-income or developing economies	0.30	0.9	PCHHI = $6500 \div (2+0.30\times3)^{0.90}$ = US$ 2493

Data and country selection

The data set used in Part II of this report was constructed from micro-data from developed economies and emerging and developing economies. Whenever possible, data sets used combined information on individual wage and total household income. The Panel Study of Income Dynamics (PSID), a US longitudinal data set that has collected data from households since 1968, is used for all US estimates, while for European countries the EU Statistics on Income and Living Conditions (EU-SILC) is employed. EU-SILC is supported by the European Commission and has been progressively implemented since 2003. Both of these surveys provide statistics on the income and living standards of workers and their families. Whereas in the case of the EU-SILC we use data from the first available year for all countries (either 2003 or 2004), in the case of the PSID we use the available survey as of 1997. In the case of emerging and developing countries, the analysis relies on national data sources. Attempts were made to include emerging and developing countries which are members of the G20 (given their relatively large size), as well as a limited number of other countries, including poorer countries such as Peru, the Philippines and Viet Nam. Coverage of Africa is limited to South Africa due to difficulties in obtaining data sets for other countries with information on both individual wages and household income.

The data cover a pre-crisis and a post-crisis period. In practice, the exact time frame of the analysis varies by country, mostly due to constraints related to data availability. While data are available for the United States for periods before the year 2000 (in fact, we selected 1997 as the first period to be observed for the PSID), comparable data from the EU-SILC survey are available only from 2003 or 2004 for most European countries in the sample, ending in 2010. The quality of the data set also improved over time. In the analyses, 2006 is usually used as the starting point for European economies and for the United States. In the case of emerging and developing economies, where household surveys tend to be conducted less frequently, the first data point usually (but not always) lies between 2000 and 2002; the second data point lies as close as possible to the beginning of the global economic and financial crisis; the third data point is the latest available year. Most data for this group of countries cover approximately a ten-year period from 2000–02 to 2010–12.

The combined data set used for this report obviously has limitations. First, there are differences in the definitions that are used. In particular, there are variations in how "wages" are defined across countries. Similarly, countries differ in the way in which household income is defined, and in the extent to which information is provided on the different sources of non-wage income – particularly on employment-related income of the self-employed and on capital gains. Second, surveys include measurement errors related to the accuracy of information collected as well as errors in estimation that arise in the process of extrapolation to the overall population. This is the case for the data from emerging and developing economies, but also for the EU-SILC.[64] Tables A5 and A6 show the data sources and years used for emerging and developing economies. The following text describes in detail all data sources used.

Table A5 Data sources for emerging and developing economies

Region	Country	Data source
Asia	India	Employment–Unemployment Survey (EUS)
	China (1)	China Household Income Project (CHIP)
	China (2)	China Health and Nutrition Survey (CHNS)
	Indonesia	National Labour Force Survey (SAKERNAS) and National Socio-Economic Survey (SUSENAS)
	Philippines	Family Income and Expenditure Survey (FIES) and Labour Force Survey (LFS)
	Viet Nam	Household Living Standard Survey (HLSS)
Europe	Turkey	Turkish Household Labour Force Survey (HLFS) and the Household Budget Survey (HBS)
	Russian Federation	Russian Longitudinal Monitoring Survey (RLMS-HSE)
Africa	South Africa	Various
Latin America	Brazil	Pesquisa Nacional por Amostra de Domicilios (PNAD) and Pesquisa Mensal de Emprego (PME)
	Argentina	Encuesta Permanente de Hogares (EPH)
	Peru	Encuesta Nacional de Hogares sobre Condiciones de Vida y Pobreza (ENAHO)
	Chile	Encuesta de Caracterización Socioeconómica Nacional (CASEN)
	Mexico	Encuesta de Ingresos y Gastos de los Hogares (ENIGH) and Encuesta Nacional de Ocupación y Empleo (ENOE)
	Uruguay	Encuesta Continua de Hogares (ECH)

Table A6 Reference years for emerging and developing economies

Region	Country	Year 1	Year 2	Year 3
Asia	India (EUS)	1999–2000	2004–05	2011–12
	China (CHIP)	2002	2007	2009
	China (CHNS)	2004	2006	2009
	Indonesia (SAKERNAS)	2001	2005	2009
	Indonesia (SUSENAS)	2001	2005	2010
	Philippines (FIES)	2003	–	2009
	Philippines (LFS)	Jan. 2004	–	Jan. 2010
	Viet Nam (HLSS)	2002	2006	2010
Europe	Russian Federation (RLMS-HSE)	2002	2006	2012
	Turkey (HLFS)	2005	–	2010
	Turkey (HBS)	2005	–	2007
	EU-SILC	2003/04	All years	2010
Americas	US (PSID)	1997	All years	2010
	Argentina (EPH)	2003	2007	2012
	Brazil (PNAD)	2001	2007	2012
	Brazil (PME)	2001	2007	2012
	Peru (ENAHO)	2004	2008	2012
	Chile (CASEN)	2000	2006	2009
	Mexico (ENIGH)	2000	2008	2012
	Mexico (ENOE)	2000	2008	2012
	Uruguay (ECH)	2004	2008	2012
Africa	South Africa	2002	2007	2011
	South Africa	2000	2005	2010

Sample selection criteria

All data sets have been cleaned of inconsistencies and outliers and have been trimmed according to sample selection criteria applied equally to all data sets. The selection criteria are summarized below, showing that we eliminate very young dependent households and households whose members are elderly, in the sense that they do not have links to labour market activities.

Selection at the level of the individual applies the following criteria:

- Anyone 15 years old or younger is excluded. However, if a child 15 or younger has income, the income is included as part of the household income before they are dropped from the sample. This ensures their income is not excluded from total household income.
- Anyone classified as a full-time student or reporting inability to work due to a disability is excluded. These individuals are usually classified as "out of the labour force" (OLF), but differ from other people classified as "OLF" because they are not ready to become active participants.
- Anyone 64 or older who is unemployed or out of the labour force is excluded because they are not potential labour market participants.

These three categories of individuals are dropped in order to limit the sample to individuals who are potential labour market participants. However, in so far as at least one member of these individuals' households is not excluded on the basis of the above criteria, the household remains part of the sample and the individuals are taken into account when estimating the equivalent scales which normalize household income. For example, a household with two people over 64 is completely excluded from the individual and household samples. By contrast, in a family with two working adults and two children under 15, the children are dropped from the individual sample, but a family of four is retained for the purpose of estimating per capita values, for example, per capita household income.

Once the selection is completed at the individual level, sample selection criteria at the household level are applied as follows:

- If *all* members of the household are at least 70 years old, the household is excluded even if one or more household members claim to be employed.
- If *all* members of the household are at least 65 years old and all household members are unemployed or out of the labour force, the household is excluded.
- If *all* members of the household are 18 years old or younger the household is excluded even if one or more household members claim to be employed.

Europe (EU-SILC data)

For most countries in Europe, EU-SILC data are used. Data are available for 29 countries from either 2003 or 2004 to 2010, and available only for the last year (2010) for Croatia and Switzerland. Table A7 shows the distribution of the sample of individuals aged 16 and above by country and for each of the available years. Table A8 shows the same distribution once we have weighted the data

Table A7 Distribution of the complete sample, by country and year

	2003	2004	2005	2006	2007	2008	2009	2010
Austria	7944	8969	10044	11120	9037	9007	9357	9258
Belgium	8404	8198	9504	10305	10031	9769	9676	9368
Bulgaria				8714	8568	10757	11805	12349
Cyprus		7911	7681	7390	7023	6440	7805	8164
Czech Republic		7140	12138	15669	18240	15875	14638	14022
Denmark	11840	10350	9833	9939	9809	9973	9865	9021
Estonia	7871	8472	11436	10552	9477	9796	9604	9473
Finland	20264	20436	19513	19221	18499	17376	18659	15827
France	15851	15464	16080	16671	16407	16395	16975	17246
Germany		20336	20585	20337	18475	18132	17985	18366
Greece	11578	10085	10260	9976	11348	12017	11652	9711
Hungary	0	12322	13623	15453	15552	17692	17510	20915
Iceland	6124	6125	5993	6033	6061	5956	6198	6332
Ireland	9035	9644	9006	8477	7839	7846	7064	
Italy	43180	39149	37914	36604	36085	35070	32805	32744
Latvia		6697	7627	7712	9126	10144	10698	11004
Lithuania	0	8574	8502	8996	8523	9086	9508	8860
Luxembourg	6828	6809	7039	7170	6903	7645	9032	10099
Malta						7153	7250	7827
Netherlands		15294	15059	17078	16798	15475	16200	16595
Norway	10907	10729	10062	10356	9613	9343	9002	7908
Poland		33376	32537	30940	29716	27639	26813	26280
Portugal	9936	9000	8503	8230	8218	8789	8783	9606
Romania				14040	13368	12910	12633	12352
Slovakia		11504	11118	11171	12513	12361	12567	11911
Slovenia		21976	24853	22596	22614	22837	22597	21916
Spain	26024	25980	23963	24429	25490	26178	26143	24274
Sweden	9479	10235	11430	12135	12627	12479	11881	11052
Switzerland								11801
United Kingdom		16425	15000	13968	13400	12239	11648	11663
Total	**205265**	**361200**	**369303**	**395282**	**391360**	**396379**	**396353**	**395944**

Table A8 The representativeness of the sample (age 16+ in the population)

	2003	2004	2005	2006	2007	2008	2009	2010
Austria	5597232	5649314	5670950	5687390	5726730	5716189	5723961	5753396
Belgium	6751946	6670720	6942917	6993240	6994613	7077395	7121209	7176987
Bulgaria				5684380	5667859	5609350	5573473	5504147
Cyprus		523401	545389	557187	565793	574370	590138	611008
Czech Republic		7322981	7365339	7372667	7379933	7428375	7499729	7482708
Denmark	3487881	3493736	3493793	3510353	3522106	3539082	3563854	3572783
Estonia	942109	951610	957181	955684	952350	952029	942034	937957
Finland	3429718	3445352	3438060	3438522	3469620	3465694	3486422	3490489
France	37851332	38310760	38668663	38943543	39397381	39407615	39710294	39567631
Germany		54518208	54283658	54206957	54282903	54003247	53752484	53826717
Greece	7493085	7544536	7718533	7790411	7808242	7772145	7800858	7719678
Hungary		6986437	6920024	6967616	7054029	7083447	7062469	7028618
Iceland	188631	192043	197221	202988	208924	211886	205694	204745
Ireland	2795589	2841963	2922451	3013154	3058078	3051117	2996762	
Italy	40241144	40615317	40669399	40823417	41029380	41385289	41394924	41557786
Latvia		1577329	1614839	1604107	1625830	1657945	1636205	1470164
Lithuania		2351874	2351535	2392374	2404195	2396573	2368299	2282816
Luxembourg	305234	306183	305085	308921	315649	327431	339807	346174
Malta						291424	297186	297763
Netherlands		10772921	10757195	10823451	10860751	10895563	10932940	10879193
Norway	3041891	3015522	2789622	3092780	3133467	3186122	3221840	3244176
Poland		27287345	28419961	28730734	28832966	26335436	26288537	27788140
Portugal	7496615	7538436	7566542	7563214	7579329	7476115	7468328	7427838
Romania				15824847	15525148	15299138	15643709	15620096
Slovakia		3934644	3889183	3996472	4005149	4084888	4126486	4115668
Slovenia		1438142	1479054	1431650	1420372	1443380	1432298	1422322
Spain	30224324	31393743	31875154	32453037	33099238	33495288	33499766	33232906
Sweden	5738184	5859729	5792423	5821601	5939728	5975676	6024878	6090490
Switzerland								5845888
United Kingdom		39153157	40093360	40186920	40707465	40971270	41132755	41345583
Total	**155584915**	**313695403**	**316727531**	**340377617**	**342567228**	**341113479**	**341837339**	**345843867**

using cross-section weights that render the sample representative of the underlying population. Both tables show the numbers of individuals (and their representation in the population) after the sample was cleaned of inconsistencies and outliers, and once the selected sample selection criteria mentioned above were applied.

EUROSTAT provides annual income measures and asks individuals to declare the number of months they worked full time and part time during the reference income period (RIP). The RIP is always the last calendar year. Using Atkinson's[65] conversion of part-time to full-time months, the number of full-time equivalent months worked (FTMW) per year is estimated for each individual who claims to have worked at least one month during the RIP. The FTMW equals the sum of total full-time months and part-time months, where part-time months are normalized by the relative weight of part-time hours to full-time hours. Dividing total gross annual earnings by FTMW provides an estimate of gross monthly wage for employees or monthly earnings in the case of the self-employed.

Europe (non-EU-SILC data)

For the **Russian Federation**, the analysis was based on the Russian Longitudinal Monitoring Survey (RLMS-HSE).[66] The RLMS-HSE is conducted by the Higher School of Economics and ZAO "Demoscope" in cooperation with the Carolina Population Center, University of North Carolina at Chapel Hill in the United States, and the Russian Academy of Sciences' Institute of Sociology. The RLMS-HSE is nationally representative and is used because none of the regular official surveys contains information on wages and household income. The Russian Labour Force Survey provides information on employment but does not include questions on wages. The Russian Household Budget Survey does not collect information on household income: it focuses exclusively on household expenditure and does not allow for different sources of income to be distinguished from each other. Data are from 2002, 2006 and 2012. Gorodnichenko, Sabirianova and Stolyarov conclude that the "RLMS appears to be a reliable data source for examining the inequality trends in labor market outcomes, reported income, [and] consumption, with the common caveats of income underreporting and underrepresentation of the super-rich" (Gorodnichenko, Sabirianova and Stolyarov, 2010). The World Bank also favours the RLMS over official data sources in a number of publications on inequality and poverty (e.g. World Bank, 1999).

For **Turkey**, two sources of data are used. The first is the Turkish Household Labour Force Survey (HLFS), which is conducted quarterly. The years 2005 and 2010 are used for the analyses. The HLFS has data on wages alone. The second source of data is the Household Budget Survey (HBS) for 2005 and 2007. These data were also used by Tansel and Bircan and offer a much richer set of variables on income than the HLFS (Tansel and Bircan, 2010).

Asian countries

Data for **China** are from two separate sources. The first source is the China Household Income Project (CHIP) for 2002, 2007 and 2009. The surveys are nationally representative and samples were randomly drawn from the larger annual national household income survey conducted by the National Bureau of Statistics (NBS). The purpose of these surveys is to estimate wages, employment, consumption and related economic issues in both rural and urban areas of China. Data on migrants are included in this survey. The second source is the China Health and Nutrition Survey (CHNS), a longitudinal survey jointly conducted by the Carolina Population Center at the University of North Carolina at Chapel Hill in the United States, and the National Institute of Nutrition and Food Safety at the Chinese Center for Disease Control and Prevention in China. The survey covers nine provinces of varying levels of development (Helongjiang, Liaoning, Shangdong, Henan, Hubei, Hunan, Jiangsu, Guangxi, Guizhou provinces) for 2004, 2006 and 2009.

The analysis for **India** is based on the Employment–Unemployment Survey (EUS) carried out by the National Sample Survey Office (NSSO) of India. It covers all major Indian states. The years (known as rounds) considered for the analyses are the 55th (July 1999 to June 2000), 61st (July 2004 to June 2005) and 68th (July 2011 to June 2012). The 55th and 68th rounds do not contain information on income from self-employment. In the 61st round there is no direct question related to self-employment income, but two questions related to remuneration were introduced: (1) whether respondents regarded their current income from self-employment as remunerative (as opposed to being produced for self-consumption), based on different income brackets; and (2) what amount per month they would consider remunerative (as opposed to being produced for self-consumption). From these questions, it would have been possible to compute approximate averages for each income bracket, but this procedure was considered inappropriate for the analyses undertaken for this study. Therefore, income from self-employment and total employment-related income are not computed.

The statistics for **Indonesia** are based on two different sources. The main source is the national labour force survey (Survei angkatan kerja nasional, SAKERNAS). This provides the basis for calculation of all statistics related to employment, wages, income from self-employment and household employment-related income. The years 2001, 2005 and 2009 are used for the analyses. Even though more recent SAKERNAS data are available, these could not be considered since the questionnaire has undergone changes and the self-employed are no longer questioned about their income. SAKERNAS does not contain income from sources other than employment and consequently household income cannot be calculated. Therefore, the national socio-economic survey (Survei social ekonomi nasional, SUSENAS), a household survey, was taken into consideration as a second source of data. It contains information on household income based on a consumption approach and is available for 2001, 2005 and 2010.

Data for the **Philippines** are taken from two data sets, the Family Income and Expenditure Survey (FIES) and the Labour Force Survey (LFS). The years 2003 and 2009 are used from the FIES, and for the LFS the second (July 2003), third (October 2003), and fourth (January 2004) quarters of 2003; the second (July 2009), third (October 2009), and fourth (January 2010) quarters of 2009; and the first (April 2011), second (July 2011), and third (October 2011) quarters of 2011 are employed. The LFS contains data on wages but not income from self-employment. Income from self-employment is covered in the FIES. Thus, wages are taken from the LFS, whereas income from self-employment is taken from the FIES. Total employment-related income is computed using both surveys. Statistics on household income are taken from the FIES, which collects income data at the household level. Given that FIES data were unavailable for 2011, the 2011 analysis covers wages, but excludes income from self-employment and household income.

Data on **Viet Nam** are from the Household Living Standard Surveys (HLSS) for 2002, 2006 and 2010. The Labour and Employment Survey (LES) is not used because in recent years (i.e. 2011 and 2012) the self-employed have not been asked about their income from self-employment.

Americas

For **Argentina**, we use the Encuesta Permanente de Hogares (EPH). The survey includes demographic and socio-economic characteristics of the population and is linked to the labour force. It is implemented by INDEC (Instituto Nacional de Estadísticas y Censos) and is used in our analyses for 2003, 2007 and 2012. Micro-data are available for 31 urban areas (*aglomerados urbanos*).

For **Brazil**, micro-data are used from two surveys: the Pesquisa Nacional por Amostra de Domicilios (PNAD) and the Pesquisa Mensal de Emprego (PME). Both surveys are conducted by the Instituto Brasileiro de Geografia e Estadística (IBGE). Given that the PME collects information only on wages and on income from self-employment, other forms of income were imputed using the PNAD in order to estimate total household income (following the methodology by Machado and Perez Ribas, 2010). Data are used for 2001, 2007 and 2012.

For **Chile**, data are from the Encuesta de Caracterización Socioeconómica Nacional (CASEN), which is carried out every two or three years. Data are used for 2000, 2006 and 2011.

For **Mexico**, the Encuesta de Ingresos y Gastos de los Hogares (ENIGH) is used; this collects information on the distribution, levels and structure of household incomes and expenditures, together with information on the economic activities of these households. We use data for 2002, 2008 and 2012.

For **Peru**, the Encuesta Nacional de Hogares sobre Condiciones de Vida y Pobreza (ENAHO) is used. It has been conducted since 1995 by the Instituto Nacional de Estadística e Informática (INEI) and is national. Data are used for 2004, 2008, and 2012.

For the **United States**, the Panel Study of Income dynamics (PSID) is used. This is a longitudinal dataset, compiled annually from 1968 to 1996 and biannually from 1997 onwards. In relation to previous years, the 1997 sampling strategy changed significantly in order to reduce the cost of collecting the data. Thus, 1997 was the year that was both as far back as possible in time and also the best in terms of attaining a sample comparable to years ahead in time, e.g. the post-crisis periods close to 2010. Despite becoming biannual, the PSID has kept the main characteristics of a longitudinal study in that it keeps on tracking families previously surveyed, new families that branch out from previously surveyed families (e.g. children who later form families of their own, divorced parents who create new households, etc.). However, our interest is not in tracking the same families but in interpreting income distributions over periods. This is why we have chosen to use the cross-sectional data of the PISD, which is also available by selecting the appropriate sample weights. Each household in the sample is represented by the head and (where applicable) the spouse. All other household members are accounted for (e.g. their wages, social security contributions, capital gains etc.); although we cannot identify their individual characteristics, this is not a drawback and has no adverse effect for our analytical purposes. The core sample includes socio-economic variables collected continuously over time with extensive and complete information on labour market outcomes and required household characteristics, among others. The PSID is directed by the University of Michigan, and the data are used by researchers, policy analysts and teachers around the globe. According to the PSID website, the National Science Foundation recognized the PSID as one of the 60 most significant advances funded by the NSF in its 60-year history.

For **Uruguay**, the Encuesta Continua de Hogares, implemented by the Instituto Nacional de Estadística (INE), is used for 2004, 2008 and 2012. However, while the data for 2008 and 2012 cover both urban and rural areas, those for 2004 cover only urban areas.

Africa

For **South Africa**, different data sets are used for the labour market and household income indicators since there is no single nationally representative survey for the appropriate period which includes enough detailed information on all variables. The labour force survey is used for 2002 (Q2), 2007 (Q2) and 2012 (Q4), and the income and expenditure survey for 2000, 2006 and 2010/11.

Appendix III

Changes in household income inequality

Inequality estimates using counterfactuals

To isolate the impact of changing wage inequality on household income inequality, the analysis relies on estimating a counterfactual outcome where the latter holds inequality constant in the first period (e.g. in the pre-crisis period). Counterfactuals simulate the unknown and aim to answer the question "What would have happened if …?". For example, in this exercise, one question the simulation aims to answer is what would have happened to household income inequality between two periods of time (e.g. before and after the crisis) if wage inequality had remained constant between the two periods. The method of counterfactuals isolates wage inequality while identifying how changes in other sources of income (social transfers, income from self-employment, etc.) contribute to the observed (as opposed to simulated) change in household income inequality between two periods. To see this more clearly, the difference in the *D9/D*1 between 2010 (*T*2) and 2006 (*T*1) can be interpreted with the following expression:

$$\Delta_{T1,T2}D91 = \Delta_{T1,T2}D91(wages) + \Delta_{T1,T2}D91(other\ incomes) \qquad (1)$$

Expression (1) shows that different sources of income can contribute to changes of the D9/D1 ratio between two periods. Let $\Delta_{T1,T2}D91^{C,WG}$ be the change in the D9/D1 ratio between the actual outcome and the counterfactual – based on per capita household income.[67] In other words, $\Delta_{T1,T2}D91^{C,WG}$ is the ratio that would have resulted if wage inequality in 2010 (*T*2) was measured allowing for wage inequality to be the same in 2006 (*T*1):

$$\begin{aligned}
&\Delta_{T1,T2}D91 = \Delta_{T1,T2}D91(wages) + \Delta_{T1,T2}D91(others\ incomes)\\
&\Delta_{T1,T2}D91^{C,WG} = \Delta_{T1,T2}D91(wages)^{C} + \Delta_{T1,T2}D91(others\ incomes) \qquad (2)\\
\Rightarrow &\left(\Delta_{T1,T2}D91 - \Delta_{T1,T2}D91^{C,WG}\right) = \Delta_{T1,T2}D91(wages) - \Delta_{T1,T2}D91(wages)^{C}
\end{aligned}$$

Expression (2) shows that by construction, the effect of wage inequality has been isolated from household income inequality between two periods. In practice and by construction the distance $\Delta_{T1,T2}D91(wages)^{C}$ should equal zero (because changes in wage inequality are held constant over time) such that the final expression in (2) uses $(\Delta_{T1,T2}D91 - \Delta_{T1,T2}D91^{C,WG})$ to evaluate changes in household income inequality which result from changing wage inequality.[68] The same exercise can be applied to any of the other income components identified at individual level to isolate their effect on household income inequality, for example, to isolate the effect of changing dispersion in unemployment benefits or self-employment income.

Appendix IV

Decomposing wage gaps

To calculate the wage gaps for different pairs of population subgroups (e.g. women and men, migrants and nationals, informal economy and formal economy workers), the following methodology was employed.

Calculating the explained and unexplained parts of unadjusted wage gaps

First, the 1st, 2nd, 3rd, … , 8th and 9th deciles of the wage distribution are calculated using wage employees only and for each subgroup separately (males, females, migrants, nationals, formal economy workers, informal economy workers). In each case, the wage distribution is based on a full-time equivalent measure of monthly wages for countries where the data is provided annually (European Union economies and the United States) and declared monthly wages for all other data sets (emerging and developing economies). In all cases, our analysis applies only to the last available year. The last year is always 2010 for developed economies and 2011 or 2012 for emerging and developing economies. The nine estimated deciles are pairwise compared between each set of mutually exclusive subgroups of employees. In our comparison, and for each paired subgroup, we define one of the subgroups to be the "disadvantaged" group in relation to their returns in the labour market. Among the subgroups considered, females, migrants and informal economy workers are considered disadvantaged whereas males, nationals and formal economy workers are considered, on average, to fare better in the labour market when compared to their corresponding disadvantaged groups.

Let the disadvantaged subgroup be $G0$ and the advantaged subgroup be $G1$. The decile-specific "raw" wage gap is the wage decile difference between $G0$ and $G1$. Thus, if we define a decile of the wage distribution as $V_g(\alpha)$, $g=1, 0$ such that $\alpha=1,2,3,\ldots,8,9$ then $v_{0,1}(\alpha)=v_1(\alpha)-v_0(\alpha)$ is the raw difference of the α-decile between pairs of mutually exclusive subgroups.

The explained and unexplained parts of the gaps are then calculated. In general terms, the "explained part" takes into account differences between the two groups being compared based on labour market characteristics observed in the data, namely, experience, education (four categories), occupational category (managerial, highly skilled, semi-skilled, low-skilled and unskilled), economic activity (from manufacturing to services, about ten categories including public administration), location (urban, rural) and work intensity (hours worked). When experience is missing, age is considered as a proxy.[69] The unexplained part of the decomposition then captures wage difference that cannot be explained by the previous list of variables.

How are the explained and the unexplained parts technically identified? Let $v_c(\alpha)$ be the "counterfactual" decile to the subgroup $G0$ (i.e. the α-decile from a hypothetical distribution of wages that would be observed for the disadvantaged subgroup $G0$ if they were to receive the same returns to their observed labour market characteristics as those received by their counterfactuals in the advantaged subgroup $G1$). To identify the counterfactual distribution for subgroup $G0$, we employ propensity score matching. In other words, a conditional probability model is employed to compare each member of disadvantaged subgroup $G0$ to all members in the advantaged subgroup $G1$ in terms of their observable characteristics. Then each individual in the $G0$ subgroup is assigned the wages of the individual in the advantaged subgroup $G1$ that is closest to him or her in terms of propensity-score weighted labour market characteristics. The distribution of assigned wages becomes the counterfactual wage distribution for the sub-group $G0$, i.e., the disadvantaged one.[70]

For each decile the following difference is estimated:

The distance $\{v_1(\alpha)-v_c(\alpha)\}$ is the decile-specific difference between the wages of the advantaged group and the wages that the disadvantaged group would have obtained if they had had the same returns to all of their observable characteristics. In other words, this is the wages of the *advantaged* subgroup minus the counterfactual wages of the *disadvantaged* subgroup and identifies the explained part of the wage gap. To calculate the unexplained wage gap, the following calculation is made: $\{v_c(\alpha)-v_0(\alpha)\}$. This equation is the counterfactual wages of the disadvantaged subgroup minus the actual wages of the subgroup. Together, $\{v_1(\alpha)-v_c(\alpha)\} + \{v_c(\alpha)-v_0(\alpha)\}$, i.e. the explained and the unexplained parts, add up to the raw (overall) decile-specific wage gap. The explained and/or unexplained parts can be positive or negative. When the explained part is negative it indicates that at that specific decile, and in accordance with the labour market characteristics X, the wages of the disadvantaged subgroup should be higher relative to the labour market characteristics of the advantaged subgroup in the same decile, i.e. the disadvantaged subgroup is overqualified with regard to X in that decile. When the unexplained part is negative, it indicates positive discrimination towards the disadvantaged subgroup with regard to the set X of covariates. The sum of the explained and unexplained parts yields the total unadjusted pay gap.

Notes

Part I. Major trends in wages

1 For detailed description of macroeconomic effects, see Lavoie and Stockhammer, 2013.

2 The IMF considered that in Germany, in light of the strong labour market, "it would not be inappropriate for real wages to rise, and therefore help improve the labor share of national income. This would help spur domestic demand, and make the economy less vulnerable to external shocks, while not endangering Germany's competitiveness" (IMF, 2013a, p. 24). The IMF similarly called for increases in basic wages in Japan, "which would be important to stimulate inflation expectations and support purchasing power once inflation starts to rise" (IMF, 2013b, p. 12). Underlying this call is a view that the dwindling labour share of income has forced Japanese workers to dip into their savings to finance consumption growth, and that higher wages are required for a transition towards sustainable growth led by the private sector (Botman and Jakab, 2014).

3 In the light of the cyclical and structural factors affecting the labour market, the US Federal Reserve Bank is also looking towards changes in compensation as part of its overall evaluation of labour market slack (and subsequently monetary policy). See Yellen, 2014.

4 "Indeed, real product wages – a measure of wages relative to the prices that companies charge for their output – fell broadly in line with output per worker. That could reflect companies responding to faltering output per worker by bearing down on pay. But the observed combination of weak wages and lower output per worker could also reflect people becoming more willing to accept pay restraint, encouraging companies to employ more people" (Bank of England, 2013, p. 34).

5 "Forecasters significantly underestimated the increase in unemployment and the decline in private consumption and investment associated with fiscal consolidation" (Blanchard and Leigh, 2013, p. 5).

6 See e.g. ILO, 2014e.

7 The G20 includes: Argentina, Australia, Brazil, Canada, China, France, Germany, India, Indonesia, Italy, Japan, the Republic of Korea, Mexico, the Russian Federation, Saudi Arabia, South Africa, Turkey, the United Kingdom, the United States and the European Union.

8 This is calculated as the sum of GDP of the 19 individual countries that are members of the G20 (the 20th member being the European Union) as a share of the world's GDP, based on purchasing power parity, as estimated in IMF, 2013c.

9 According to recent ILO estimates, in 2014 there are 3.2 billion employed persons in the world, of which 1.6 billion (50.3%) are waged and salaried workers (ILO, 2013a).

10 Data are available from the ILO Global Wage Database (see box 2). The average wage has been adopted as an ILO "decent work indicator" (ILO, 2012b).

11 These elements can also be captured by other measures of productivity, such as output per hour worked (another definition of labour productivity), capital productivity and multifactor productivity. Capital productivity is another partial measure of productivity which reflects capital's contribution to changes in production. Multifactor productivity "helps disentangle the direct growth contributions of labour, capital, intermediate inputs and technology. This is an important tool for reviewing past growth patterns and for assessing the potential for future economic growth" (OECD, 2001, p. 20). However, some research questions the accuracy and relevance of using multifactor productivity (Felipe, 2008; Felipe and McCombie, 2013).

12 Moreover, labour productivity "forms a direct link to a widely used measure of living standards, income per capita", and is "important as a reference statistic in wage bargaining" (OECD, 2001, p. 15). It is also a decent work indicator.

13 Considering the full sample of 33 countries used in figure 8, trends in labour compensation and wage growth vis-à-vis productivity growth changed (based on choice of "wage" variable and deflator) for slightly more than one-third of countries. However, as shown in the figure, the measure used does not affect the final results. Using wages and the CPI, about half the countries experienced wage growth that exceeded productivity growth over the period. When compensation and the GDP deflator are used, the findings are similar (See Sobeck, forthcoming).

14 See OECD, 2012a, and the shift-share analysis in ILO, 2010a. In the financial sector, rising profits were accompanied by higher bonuses and wages, but not for everyone. Bell and Van Reenen showed that the premium attached to being employed in the UK financial sector increased only for the top 10 per cent of earners in the sector (Bell and Van Reenen, 2013). Looking at over 400 UK listed companies from 1999 to 2010, the authors also showed that higher shareholder returns are strongly associated with the level of pay of CEOs and senior executives, an order of magnitude smaller for managers, and practically non-existent for other workers. According to the authors, the median pay of a FTSE-100 CEO in the United Kingdom is now about 116 times that of the median worker, compared to a ratio of 11 in 1980. In the United States, the median pay of an S&P 500 CEO has risen to 240 times that of the median worker in 2008 from 26 times in 1970.

15 For a more detailed description, see ILO, 2010a, Technical Appendix II.

16 For example, in South Africa the only source of data on the average wage is the Quarterly Employment Statistics, whose most recent available data relates to March 2006 and covers only employees in the formal, non-agricultural business sector. In China, the wage series refers to so-called urban units, a category that comprises mostly state-owned and collective-owned enterprises, and excludes part of the private sector; a new series for wages in private enterprises was started in 2008, but no series currently combines both the public and the private sectors. In India, representative data are available only through special computations using the National Sample Survey Office (NSSO) employment/unemployment data. Different official sources of wage data exist, including the Annual Survey of Industries (ASI), the Employment–Unemployment Survey and the Wage Rate Index, which is computed from the occupational wage survey with panel data from about 1,256 units covering 14 manufacturing industries, four mining industries and three plantations. This source was used in the ILO *Global Wage Report 2012/13* after consultation with the Ministry of Statistics and Programme Implementation; this edition of the report has switched to the NSSO due to its broader coverage.

17 PALMS, a collaboration between the University of Cape Town and the University of Michigan, has painstakingly assembled and harmonized the entire sequence of existing labour market surveys carried out by Statistics South Africa since 1994, including the October Household Surveys (1994–99), the biannual Labour Force Surveys (2000–07) and the Quarterly Labour Force Surveys (since 2008) (see Wittenberg, 2014).

18 A recently adopted report on productivity measurement produced by a task team from the National Economic Development and Labour Council (NEDLAC) in South Africa put forth measures to improve labour productivity measurement.

19 PPP$1 is equivalent to the purchasing power of US$1 in the United States. For example, if you were to travel to the United States from China and walk into a bank to exchange 3,000 yuan for US dollars, the bank would give you about US$490. However, in terms of purchasing power in China, 3,000 yuan is equivalent to about US$1,140, because it is less expensive to live in China than in the United States.

Part II. Wages and income inequality

20 The OECD has published a number of reports on the subject: see e.g. OECD, 2008; OECD, 2011; OECD, 2014a. Taking a perspective from developing countries, at least two of the World Bank's last ten *World Development Reports* centred on issues related to inequality: see World Bank, 2006; World Bank, 2012. The IMF also recently studied the link between income inequality, economic growth and fiscal policy (see e.g. Berg and Ostry, 2011; IMF, 2014b). The ILO itself has issued various publications on inequality: see e.g. ILO and IILS, 2008; ILO, 2014b. These institutional reports have been published alongside a growing number of academic articles and books on inequality, including (to name just a few) Piketty, 2013; Milanovic, 2011; and Galbraith, 2012. The growing academic research has also been summarized in large volumes such as Salverda, Nolan and Smeeding, 2009a.

21 This is also true within countries. Chetty, Hendren, Kline and Saez show for example that in the United States, areas of high social mobility are also places which have, among several things, less income inequality: see Chetty, Hendren, Kline and Saez, 2014.

22 See, for example, the literature reviews in Neves and Silva, 2014. In principle, inequality may accelerate growth, for instance by providing incentive for innovation and entrepreneurship (Lazear and Rosen, 1981) or by allowing some individuals to accumulate enough capital to start a business and invest in education (Barro, 2000). At the same time, inequality may have a negative impact on growth by negatively affecting human capital investment of underprivileged individuals (Perotti, 1996) or by generating economic and political instability that reduces investment (Alesina and Perotti, 1996; Rodrik, 1999).

23 See in particular page 155.

24 However, fiscal redistribution is also limited in as much as the labour market is dominated by the informal sector. For example, in the case of Turkey, the fiscal reforms in 2007 and 2008 reduced wage inequality, as they targeted low income earners by reducing the tax wedge and social security costs among low income earners (Gönenç and Rawdanowicz, 2010). However, despite the effect such reforms had among workers in the formal sector, the size of the informal sector in Turkey remains significant at about 40 per cent of the working age population (Tansel and Kan, 2012).

25 According to the Canberra Group, an expert group mandated to provide conceptual and definitional guidance to national statistical offices, "total income" and "disposable income" are the main income aggregates produced (UNECE, 2011, p. 17). The components of total household income are set out in figure A1 (see Appendix II); disposable income is obtained by deducting from total income all current transfers paid, such as direct taxes and social insurance contributions. *Disposable income* is usually the preferred measure to analyse income distribution, but it is less frequently available than *total income*, including in our own data set. Hence this report studies trends in total household income rather than disposable household income.

26 For practical purposes, this report has selected as thresholds the 30th and 70th percentiles of the household income distribution to identify households in the middle class. Whereas the proportion of households between these thresholds remains constant at 40 per cent, the incomes that define the upper and lower limits can change to become either wider apart (thereby stretching the income values associated with the middle class) or closer together (thereby compressing the income range identified with middle-class households). Another interesting measure of inequality includes the top 10 per cent versus the bottom 40 per cent, which was found to be quite robust and highly correlated with another possible measure of inequality: the Gini coefficient (Cobham and Sumner, 2013).

27 Since as early as the 1980s, most developed economies have experienced increasing household income inequality: the gap between the top and bottom

10 per cent widened in countries where inequality was already high, such as the United Kingdom and the United States. This was also the case in countries with low inequality, such as Germany and the Nordic countries. Thus, between 1985 and 2007/08 the Gini coefficient increased from 34 to 44 in the United States and from 32 to 35 in the United Kingdom; likewise, in the same period the Gini coefficient increased from 20 to 26 in Sweden, from 23 to 25 in Norway and from 21 to 26 in Finland. In the case of emerging and developing economies, there has been no universal trend: estimates from 40 emerging and developing economies show that in 13 countries inequality has increased, in six countries inequality has not changed significantly, and the remaining 21 countries have experienced a significant decline in inequality (Ferreira and Ravallion, 2009). Some examples of emerging and developing economies where inequality has decreased substantially from the mid-1990s to the mid-2000s are (as measured by the Gini coefficient) Chile (3.3 per cent), Mexico (4.1 per cent) and Turkey (8.1 per cent) (OECD, 2011).

28 Note that in Greece inequality has increased in 2011 and 2012, according to Eurostat, http://appsso.eurostat.ec.europa.eu/nui/show.do?dataset=ilc_di12&lang=en

29 Note that for China, different data sources indicate different trends particularly in the years between the early 2000s and 2006/07, where data from the China Health and Nutrition Survey (CHNS) show a decline in inequality while data from the China Household Income Project (CHIP) point towards increasing inequality. Both data sources suggest that inequality declined in most recent years.

30 Although estimates from Turkey could not be directly integrated in the data due to significant difference in the structure of the data, our estimates for Turkey also suggest a decrease in wage inequality among formal sector wage employees when comparing both D9/D1 and D5/D1. The decrease, however, had only a mild effect on household income inequality.

31 For the technical definition of household income, see Appendix II.

32 In the estimation of the "counterfactual", we hold wages constant and allow for the dispersion (inequality) of other incomes and total income to vary between periods. It is important to point out that in this case we are assuming exogeneity between changes in the dispersion of wages and the dispersion of all other income components. Clearly, if other incomes (in particular, social transfers) change endogenously with wages at each decile of the distribution, our counterfactual would not be a pure way of keeping the distribution of wages constant: the movement of other components would have some of the effect of movement in wages (Belser and Vazquez-Alvarez, forthcoming).

33 These other sources include self-employment income, social transfers, private intra-household transfers and capital gains. For detailed definitions of these other sources of household income, see notes to figure 29.

34 A decline in the wage effect does not necessarily imply a decline in wage inequality. However, ILO analyses conducted for this report show that for these countries it is the case.

35 Given that our sample excludes households where no member is of working age, the higher share of pensions in total household income in Italy and Greece may reflect the fact that in these countries more pensioners live with other family members who are of working age.

36 It must be kept in mind that households with very high incomes tend to be under-represented in household surveys, and the results presented may therefore be more representative of the incomes of the bottom 99 per cent of the population, as pointed out in Brandolini and Smeeding, 2009, p. 77. Since high-income respondents may be underestimated in survey samples or may under-report capital gains, this is likely to exacerbate underestimation of the proportion represented by such gains in household income (see for example the case of South Africa, documented by Wittenberg, 2014). Note also that the reported capital gains in France, according to calculations from the SILC data set, jump from a small share – similar to that in other countries – until 2006 to around 10 per cent or more in 2007 and subsequent years. It is unclear if this is a real change or a data-related issue.

37 Note that in Germany, the Hartz reforms appear to have lessened the dualism in social policies through the merger of means-tested unemployment assistance programmes with the social assistance programme, which gave social assistance beneficiaries who were out of the labour market greater access to training programmes and job placement services, according to Clasen and Goerne, 2011.

38 In the case of China, figure 32 shows no information on social transfers. This is because in the case of China, the data set does not identify this category alone at the level of the household. Thus, all items that refer to social transfers are included in the category "other incomes". In practice, during the past 12 years, China has significantly extended various elements of their social protection system (including child and family benefits, maternity benefits, household income support, old age pensions and health care coverage). The significant increase has been reflected in a 3 per cent increase in public social protection expenditure (as a percentage of GDP) since the year 2000, with a view to moving to a more inclusive and mores sustainable growth pattern (ILO, 2014f).

39 In this context, the "unexplained" should be understood as *not accounted for* by the observed labour market characteristics listed in the paragraph. Similarly, the "explained" should be understood as *only accounting for* the observed labour market characteristics listed in the paragraph.

40 For example, the explained component of the gender wage gap may exist because women have less education; this raises further questions as to why this is the case. If, for example, this is because girls face gender discrimination in education that manifests itself through lower access to schooling and reduced attention from teachers (as compared to boys), education – captured by the explained component – is grounded in discrimination that may contribute to the unexplained component as well.

41 Half the median wage is used in Cyprus, since there is no national minimum wage in place.

42 See ILO and DSS, 2004. The 15th International Conference of Labour Statisticians (ICLS) defined the informal sector in terms of the characteristics of the production units (household unincorporated enterprises), rather than the characteristics of the jobs or the employed persons (ILO, 1993a). Employment in the informal sector was thus composed of all persons employed in informal sector enterprises. To better capture the "informalization" of employment, the 17th ICLS defined informal employment as comprising all informal jobs, whether carried out in formal sector enterprises, informal sector enterprises or households. Informal jobs in formal sector enterprises include employment that is not subject to standard labour legislation, income taxation, social protection or entitlement to certain social benefits (ILO, 2003a).

Part III. Policy responses to address wages and inequality

43 See http://www.ilo.org/global/standards/lang--en/index.htm

44 ILO's Equal Remuneration Convention, 1951 (No. 100), represents a widely agreed standard.

45 Looking at compliance rates with existing minimum wage laws in four Latin American countries (Chile, Costa Rica, Peru and Uruguay), Marinakis shows, for example, that the level of non-compliance is particularly high in rural areas, where productivity is lower and where labour inspectorates and trade unions have a much weaker presence (Marinakis, 2014).

46 ILO, forthcoming.

47 ILO, 2014f.

48 The ILO's Social Protection Floors Recommendation, 2012 (No. 202), provides guidance to member States in building comprehensive social security systems and extending social security coverage by prioritizing the establishment of national floors of social protection. To achieve universal coverage of populations, the ILO's extension strategy recommends ensuring at least basic levels of income security and access to health care as a priority through nationally defined social protection floors while progressively ensuring a wider scope and higher levels of protection.

Appendix I

49 Formerly known as the Conditions of Work and Employment Programme (TRAVAIL).

50 ILO-commissioned report: Mehran, 2010. Peer reviews: Tillé, 2010; Jeong and Gastwirth, 2010; Ahn, 2010.

51 Aiming for the broadest possible coverage is in line with the idea that decent work and hence adequate earnings are a concern for all workers, and that statistical indicators should cover all those to whom an indicator is relevant. See ILO, 2008b.

52 We do so on the basis of the IMF's consumer price index (CPI) for each country. In cases where our national counterparts explicitly provide a real wage series, the real wage series is used in place of the nominal series deflated by the IMF CPI.

53 Our universe includes all countries and territories for which data on employment are available from the ILO's Global Employment Trends Model (GET Model), and thus excludes some small countries and territories (e.g. the Channel Islands and the Holy See) that have no discernible impact on global or regional trends.

54 This is in line with standard survey methodology, where a model-based framework is generally used for item non-response, while a design-based framework is used for questionnaire non-response.

55 For a discussion of the missing data problem, see also ILO, 2010b, p. 8.

56 An alternative specification with GDP per capita and population size produced very similar results.

57 Data for the number of persons employed and the number of employees are from KILM (ILO, 2013a), and data on GDP in 2005 PPP$ from the World Bank's World Development Indicators.

58 The estimate, $\hat{n}_h$, of the number of employees in region h is obtained by multiplying the number of employees in countries from the region for which we have wage data with the uncalibrated weights, and then summing up across the region.

59 See for example the work done mainly for industrialized countries by the International Labor Comparisons programme of the US Bureau of Labor Statistics (2009) (http://www.bls.gov/fls/). Since we do not compare levels, but focus on change over time in individual countries, data requirements are less demanding in our context.

60 See also ILO, 2008a, p. 15 for the association between wage levels and GDP per capita. Notwithstanding this, wage developments can diverge from trends in labour productivity in the short and medium term.

Appendix II

61 Burtless, 2009.

62 OECD, 2011, p. 34.

63 According to the Canberra Group, an expert group mandated to provide conceptual and definitional guidance to national statistical offices, "total income" and "disposable income" are the main income aggregates produced (UNECE, 2011, p. 17). While total household income is reflected in figure A1, disposable income is obtained by deducting from total income all current transfers paid, such as direct taxes, social insurance contributions or other transfers. *Disposable income* is usually the preferred measure in analysing income distribution, but it is less frequently available than *total income*, including in our own data set.

64 Verma and Betti consider that comparability in the EU-SILC could be improved through greater standardization across countries in the manner in which negative, zero and very large values are treated. They also found that non-response is high to very high in various countries, which diminishes the quality of parts of the data set (Verma and Betti, 2010).

65 Atkinson uses the "current number of hours worked and declared" by each individual and estimates the median of this variable by country and gender and separately for full time and part time, i.e. *med(hours, ft)g,c* and *med(hours, pt)g,c* for each of the *c* countries and for *g* = male and female. Using these estimates, by subgroup, he constructs *atk – scale = med(hrs, pt)g,c ÷ med(hrs, ft) g,c* and multiplies – for each individual – the total number of months worked as part time by *atk – scale* which is a number in the (0,1) range.

66 See http://www.cpc.unc.edu/projects/rlms-hse, http://www.hse.ru/org/hse/rlms.

Appendix III

67 We define household income as the sum of income from wages and other incomes. The breakdown helps to illustrate the method where we hold wage inequality constant at a given period of time and allow "other" sources of household income (i.e. the sum of self-employment income, social benefits, capital gains and intra-household private transfers) to vary between periods. As above, wages refer to income received by waged employees in the household. The counterfactual for each individual is estimated using wage distributions at individual level and the result is incorporated into the corresponding distributions of household incomes. For more detail, see DiNardo, Fortin and Lemieux, 1996, and Daly and Valetta, 2004. For a more detailed explanation of the components of household income and our estimation of per capita household income, see Appendix II.

68 That is, the measure $\Delta_{T1,T2}D91(wages)^C$ is equal to $\Delta D91(wage\ counterfactual\ to\ T1) - \Delta D91_{T1}$ where the counterfactual "mimics" the ranking and dispersion of D9/D1 in T1. In other words, the ratios $D9/D1_{T1}$ and $D9/D1)_{T2(wage\ counterfactual\ to\ T1)}$

should be equal. In practice they can vary slightly in a ranking process that maps workers ranked in *T*2 to a population in *T*1 that differs in size in the sample.

Appendix IV

69 The selected set of variables to explain returns to participation follow the classic Mincer selection in the empirical evaluation of labour market outcomes (see Mincer, 1974).

70 We use propensity score matching. The method consists in defining a set of characteristics X in the data that describe the labour market endowments of individuals (age, education, experience, skills, occupation and work intensity measures). Using as an example the gender wage gap, these characteristics are used to estimate the conditional probability of being a female, i.e. $P(Female = 1 \mid X)$. The value of the propensity score for each female is compared in a balancing process to the propensity score estimate of all males in the sample. Those males that have an identical or similar propensity score to a female are the closest match (or matches) to the female in terms of labour market characteristics (education, experience, location, industry, etc.). Once the closest male is located for each female (the nearest neighbour), the observed male's wage serves as the counterfactual wage to that female. We tried either the closest member or functions of sets of close members (e.g. the average of the *n*-set of closer males to each female in terms of the propensity score) but the final results did not vary significantly. We selected "the closest".

Bibliography

Abraham, K.; Haltiwanger, J. 1995. "Real wages and the business cycle", in *Journal of Economic Literature*, Vol. 33, Sep., pp. 1215–64.

Agnese, P.; Sala, H. 2011. "The driving forces behind the falling labour share and persistent unemployment", in *Pacific Economic Review*, Vol. 16, No. 5, pp. 577–603.

Ahn, J. 2010. *Responses to draft ILO report "Estimation of global wage trends: Methodological issues*, mimeo (Seoul, Korea Labor Institute).

Alesina, A.; Perotti, R. 1996. "Income distribution, political instability, and investment", in *European Economic Review*, Vol. 40, No. 6, pp. 1203–28.

Alesina, A.; Rodrik, D. 1994. "Distributive politics and economic growth", in *Quarterly Journal of Economics*, Vol. 109, No. 2, pp. 465–90.

Atkinson, A.B. 2007. "The distribution of earnings in OECD countries", in *International Labour Review*, Vol. 146, No. 1–2, pp. 41–60.

Azevedo, J.P.; Davalos, M.E.; Diaz-Bonilla, C.; Atuesta, B.; Castañeda, R.A. 2013. *Fifteen years of inequality in Latin America: How have labor markets helped?* Policy Research Working Paper 6384 (Washington, DC, World Bank Gender and Equity Unit).

Bai, C.-E.; Qian, Z. 2010. "The factor income distribution in China: 1978–2007", in *China Economic Review*, Vol. 21, pp. 650–70.

Bakis, A.; Polat, S. 2013. *Wage inequality in Turkey: 2002–2010*, GIAM Working Papers 13-9 (Istanbul, Galatasaray University Economic Research Center).

Banco de España. 2014. "Un análisis de los efectos composición sobre la evolución de los salarios", in *Boletín Económico*, 02/2014, pp. 57–61.

Bank of England. 2013. *Inflation Report*, Aug. (London).

Barrett, A.; McGuinness, S.; O'Brien, M. 2012. "The immigrant earnings disadvantage across the earnings and skills distributions: The case of immigrants from the EU's new member states", in *British Journal of Industrial Relations*, Vol. 50, Issue 3, Sep. 2012, pp. 457–81.

Barro, R.J. 2000. "Inequality and growth in a panel of countries", in *Journal of Economic Growth*, Vol. 5, No. 1, pp. 5–32.

Bell, B.D.; Van Reenen, J. 2013. "Extreme wage inequality: Pay at the very top", in *American Economic Review: Papers and Proceedings*, Vol. 103, No. 3, pp. 153–57.

Belman, D.; Wolfson, P.J. 2014. *What does the minimum wage do?* (Kalamazoo, MI, W.E. Upjohn Institute for Employment Research).

Belser, P.; Vazquez-Alvarez, R. Forthcoming. *The re-distributive effect of taxes on household income inequality: A counterfactual approach*, working paper (Geneva, ILO).

Berg, J. Forthcoming. "Introduction", in J. Berg (ed.): *Labour markets, institutions and inequality: Building just societies in the 21st century* (Geneva and Cheltenham, ILO and Edward Elgar).

Berg, A.; Ostry, J.D. 2011. *Inequality and unsustainable growth: Two sides of the same coin?* Discussion Note SDN/11/08 (Washington, DC, IMF).

Bertranou, F.; Casanova, L.; Jiménez, M.; Jiménez, M. 2013. *Informality and employment quality in Argentina: Country case study on labour market segmentation*, Conditions of Work and Employment Series 49 (Geneva, ILO).

Betcherman, G. 2014. "Labor market regulations: What do we know about their impacts in developing countries?", in *World Bank Research Observer* online, 16 Apr., doi: 10.1093/wbro/lku005.

Birdsall, N.; Lustig, N.; McLeod, D. 2011. *Declining inequality in Latin America: Some economics, some politics*, Working Paper 251 (Washington, DC, Center for Global Development).

Blanchard, O.; Leigh, D. 2013. *Growth forecast errors and fiscal multipliers*, Working Paper WP/13/1 (Washington, DC, IMF).

Bloomberg. 2014. "Lagarde: US should increase the minimum wage", *Market Makers*, Bloomberg Television, 16 June, http://www.bloomberg.com/video/lagarde-u-s-should-increase-the-minimum-wage-kYnLLpMbQLGPxKD79_DYZQ.html [23 Sep. 2014].

BLS (Bureau of Labor Statistics, US Department of Labor). 2012. *International comparisons of hourly compensation costs in manufacturing*, USDL-12-2460, 19 Dec. Available at: http://www.bls.gov/news.release/pdf/ichcc.pdf [23 Sep. 2014].

Botman, D.; Jakab, Z. 2014. "Abenomics: Time for a push from higher wages", *IMFdirect*, 20 Mar. Available at: http://blog-imfdirect.imf.org/2014/03/20/abenomics-time-for-a-push-from-higher-wages/ [30 Sep. 2014].

Brandolini, A.; Smeeding, T. 2009. "Income inequality in richer and OECD countries", in W. Salverda, B. Nolan and T. Smeeding (eds), pp. 71–101.

Bryson, A. 2007. "The effect of trade unions on wages", in *Reflets et perspectives de la vie économique*, Vol. 46, Nos 2–3, pp. 33–45.

Burtless, G. 2009. "Demographic transformation and economic inequality", in W. Salverda, B. Nolan and T. Smeeding (eds), pp. 435–55.

Carneiro, A.; Portugal, P.; Varejao, J. 2013. *Catastrophic job destruction*, Discussion Paper 7670 (Bonn, IZA).

CEC (Commission of the European Communities); IMF (International Monetary Fund); OECD (Organisation for Economic Co-operation and Development); UN (United Nations); World Bank. 2009. *System of National Accounts 2008* (New York). Available at: http://unstats.un.org/unsd/nationalaccount/docs/SNA2008.pdf [24 Sep. 2014].

Chauvel, L. 2006. *Les classes moyennes à la dérive* (Paris, Seuil).

Checchi, D.; Visser, J.; van de Werfhorst, H.G. 2010. "Inequality and union membership: The influence of relative earnings and inequality attitudes", in *British Journal of Industrial Relations*, Vol. 48, No. 1, Mar., pp. 84–108.

Chen, Zhihong; Ge, Ying; Lai, Huiwen; Wan, Chi. 2013. "Globalization and gender wage inequality in China", in *World Development*, Vol. 44, Apr., pp. 256–66.

Chetty, R.; Hendren, N.; Kline, P.; Saez, E. 2014. *Where is the land of opportunity? The geography of intergenerational mobility in the United States*, Working Paper 19843, Jan. (Cambridge, MA, National Bureau of Economic Research).

Clasen, J; Goerne, A. 2011. "Exit Bismarck, enter dualism? Assessing contemporary German labour market policy," in *Journal of Social Policy*, Vol. 40 (4), pp. 795–810.

Cobham, A.; Sumner, A. 2013. *Is it all about the tails? The Palma measure of income inequality*, Working Paper No. 343 (Washington, DC, Center for Global Development).

Corak, M. 2013. "Income inequality, equality of opportunity, and intergenerational mobility", in *Journal of Economic Perspectives*, Vol. 27, No. 3, pp. 79–102.

Cornia, G.A. 2012. *Inequality trends and their determinants*, United Nations University World Institute for Development Economics Research (UNU-WIDER), Working Paper 2012/09 (Helsinki).

Daly, M.C.; Valletta, R.G. 2004. "Inequality and poverty in the United States: The effects of rising dispersion of men's earnings and changing family behaviour", in *Economica*, Vol. 73, No. 289, pp. 75–98.

Das, M.; N'Diaye, P. 2013. *Chronicle of a decline foretold: Has China reached the Lewis turning point?* Working Paper WP/13/26 (Washington, DC, IMF).

Deaton, A.; Zaidi, S. 2002. *Guidelines for constructing consumption aggregates for welfare analysis*, Living Standards Measurement Study Working Paper 135 (Washington DC, World Bank).

d'Hombres, B.; Weber, A.; Elia, L. 2012. "Literature review on income inequality and the effects on social outcomes", in *European Commission Joint Research Center Scientific and Policy Report.*

DiNardo, J.; Fortin, N.M.; Lemieux, T. 1996. "Labour market institutions and the distribution of wages, 1973–1992: A semi-parametric approach", in *Econometrica*, Vol. 64, No. 5, pp. 1001–44.

Domnisoru, C. 2014. *The largest drop in income inequality in the European Union during the Great Recession: Romania's puzzling case*, Conditions of Work and Employment Series 51 (Geneva, ILO).

Doris, A.; Sweetman, O.; O'Neill, D. 2013. *Wage flexibility and the Great Recession: The response of the Irish labour market*, Discussion Paper 7787 (Bonn, IZA).

Dormeier Freire, A. 2009. "Motorbikes against Ho Chi Minh? Or the consumption icons of a social transformation in Vietnam", in *Copenhagen Journal of Asian Studies*, Vol. 27, No. 1, pp. 67–87.

Doucouliagos, H.; Stanley, T.D. 2009. "Publication selection bias in minimum-wage research? A meta-regression analysis", in *British Journal of Industrial Relations*, Vol. 47, No. 2, June, pp. 406–28.

Downes, P.; Hanslow, K.; Tulip, P. 2014. *The effect of the mining boom on the Australian Economy*, Reserve Bank of Australia Research Discussion Paper RDP2014-08.

EC (European Commission). 2007. "The labour income share in the European Union", in *Employment in Europe 2007* (Brussels, Directorate-General for Employment, Social Affairs and Equal Opportunities), pp. 237–72.

Feldstein, M. 2008. "Did wages reflect growth in productivity?", in *Journal of Policy Modeling*, Vol. 30, No. 4, pp. 591–94.

Felipe, J. 2008. "What policy makers should know about total factor productivity", in *Malaysian Journal of Economic Studies*, Vol. 45, No. 1, pp. 1–19.

Felipe, J.; McCombie, J.S.L. 2013. *The aggregate production function and the measurement of technical change* (Northampton, MA, Edward Elgar).

Ferreira, F.H.G.; Ravallion, M. 2009. "Poverty and inequality: The global context", in W. Salverda, B. Nolan and T. Smeeding (eds), pp. 599–636.

Fleck, S.; Glaser, J.; Sprague, S. 2011. "The compensation–productivity gap: A visual essay", in *Monthly Labor Review* (Washington, DC, US Bureau of Labor Statistics), Jan., pp. 57–69.

G20. 2013. Labour and employment and finance ministers' communiqué, Moscow, 19 July. Available at: http://www.fin.gc.ca/n13/13-097-eng.asp [30 Sep. 2014].

G20. 2014a. G20 Labour and Employment Ministerial Declaration, Melbourne, 10–11 September 2014.

G20. 2014b. Communiqué Meeting of G20 Finance Ministers and Central Bank Governors, Cairns, 20–21 September 2014. Available at: https://www.g20.org/sites/default/files/g20_resources/library/Communique%20G20%20Finance%20Ministers%20and%20Central%20Bank%20Governors%20Cairns.pdf [30 Oct. 2014].

Galbraith, J.K. 2012. *Inequality and instability: A study of the world economy just before the crisis* (Oxford, Oxford University Press).

Gasparini, L.; Cruces, G.; Tornarolli, L. 2009. *Recent trends in income inequality in Latin America*, Working Paper 2009-132 (Verona, Society for the Study of Economic Inequality).

Gasparini, L.; Lustig, N. 2011. "The rise and fall of income inequality in Latin America", in J.A. Ocampo and J. Ros (eds): *Oxford handbook of Latin American economics* (Oxford, Oxford University Press), ch. 27.

Gleason, S.E. 2006. *The shadow workforce: Perspectives on contingent work in the United States, Japan, and Europe* (W.E. Upjohn Institute for Employment Research, Kalamazoo, Michigan).

Goldberg, P.; Pavcnik, N. 2007. "Distributional effects of globalization in developing countries", in *Journal of Economic Literature*, Vol. 45, No. 1 (Mar.), pp. 39–82.

Goldin, C. 2014. "A grand gender convergence: Its last chapter", in *American Economic Review*, Vol. 104, No. 4, pp. 1091–1119.

Gönenç, R.; Rawdanowicz, L. 2010. *Regulatory reforms to unlock long-term growth in Turkey*, Economics Department Working Paper 77 (Paris, OECD).

Gorodnichenko, Y.; Sabirianova, P.K.; Stolyarov, D. 2010. "Inequality and volatility moderation in Russia: Evidence from micro-level panel data on consumption and income", in *Review of Economic Dynamics*, Vol. 13, No. 1, pp. 209–37.

Grimshaw, D. 2011. *What do we know about low-wage work and low-wage workers? Analysing the definitions, patterns, causes and consequences in international perspective*, Conditions of Work and Employment Series 28 (Geneva, ILO).

Grimshaw, D.; Rubery, J. Forthcoming. *The motherhood pay gap: A review of the issues, theory and international evidence* (Geneva, ILO).

Guerriero, M. 2012. *The labour share of income around the world. Evidence from a panel data set*, Development Economics and Public Policy Working Paper Series, WP No. 32/2012 (Manchester, University of Manchester).

Hayter, S. Forthcoming. "Unions and collective bargaining", in J. Berg (ed.): *Labour markets, institutions and inequality: Building just societies in the 21st century* (Geneva and Cheltenham, ILO and Edward Elgar).

Heinze, A.; Wolf, E. 2010. "The intra-firm gender wage gap: a new view on wage differentials based on linked employer-employee data", in *Journal of Population Economics*, Vol. 23, pp. 851–79.

ILO (International Labour Office). 1966. *Resolution concerning statistics of labour cost*, adopted by the 11th International Conference of Labour Statisticians (Geneva).

ILO (International Labour Office). 1973. *Resolution concerning an integrated system of wages statistics*, adopted by the 12th International Conference of Labour Statisticians (Geneva).

ILO (International Labour Office). 1993a. *Resolution concerning statistics of employment in the informal sector*, adopted by the 15th International Conference of Labour Statisticians (Geneva).

ILO (International Labour Office). 1993b. *Resolution concerning the International Classification of Status in Employment (ISCE)*, adopted by the 15th International Conference of Labour Statisticians (Geneva).

ILO (International Labour Office). 1998. *Resolution concerning the measurement of employment related income*, adopted by the 16th International Conference of Labour Statisticians (Geneva).

ILO (International Labour Office). 2003a. *Guidelines concerning a statistical definition of informal employment*, adopted by the 17th International Conference of Labour Statisticians (Geneva).

ILO (International Labour Office). 2003b. *Resolution concerning household income and expenditure statistics*, adopted by the 17th International Conference of Labour Statisticians (Geneva).

ILO (International Labour Office). 2008a. *Global Wage Report 2008/09: Minimum wages and collective bargaining – Towards policy coherence* (Geneva).

ILO (International Labour Office). 2008b. *World of Work Report 2008: Income inequalities in the age of financial globalization* (Geneva).

ILO (International Labour Office). 2010a. *Global Wage Report 2010/11: Wage policies in times of crisis* (Geneva).

ILO (International Labour Office). 2010b. *Trends Econometric Models: A review of the methodology*, 19 Jan., Employment Trends Unit (Geneva).

ILO (International Labour Office). 2012a. *Global Wage Report 2012/13: Wages and equitable growth* (Geneva).

ILO (International Labour Office). 2012b. *Decent Work indicators: Concepts and definitions* (Geneva). Available at: http://www.ilo.org/wcmsp5/groups/public/---dgreports/---integration/documents/publication/wcms_229374.pdf [23 Sep. 2014].

ILO (International Labour Office). 2013a. *Key Indicators of the Labour Market (KILM)*, 8th edition (Geneva).

ILO (International Labour Office). 2013b. *Portugal: Tackling the jobs crisis in Portugal* (Geneva).

ILO (International Labour Office). 2014a. *Greece: Productive jobs*, Studies on Growth with Equity (Geneva).

ILO (International Labour Office). 2014b. *International Journal of Labour Research: The challenge of inequality*, Vol. 6, Issue 1 (Geneva).

ILO (International Labour Office). 2014c. *Provisional Record 13, Part I. Third item on the agenda: Information and reports on the application of Conventions and Recommendations. Report of the Committee on the Applications of Standards.* International Labour Conference, 103rd Session, Geneva. Available at: http://www.ilo.org/wcmsp5/groups/public/---ed_norm/---relconf/documents/meetingdocument/wcms_246781.pdf

ILO (International Labour Office). 2014d. *Provisional Record 13, Part I. Third item on the agenda: Information and reports on the application of Conventions and Recommendations.* International Labour Conference, 103rd Session, Geneva.

ILO (International Labour Office). 2014e. *Employment policies for sustainable recovery and development: Recurrent discussion under the ILO Declaration on Social Justice for a Fair Globalization.* Report VI, International Labour Conference, 103rd Session, Geneva. Available at: http://www.ilo.org/wcmsp5/groups/public/---ed_norm/---relconf/documents/meetingdocument/wcms_240032.pdf [30 Sep. 2014].

ILO (International Labour Office). 2014f. *World Social Protection Report 2014/15: Building economic recovery, inclusive development and social justice* (Geneva). Available at: http://www.ilo.org/wcmsp5/groups/public/---dgreports/---dcomm/documents/publication/wcms_245201.pdf; http://www.social-protection.org/gimi/gess/ShowTheme.action?th.themeId=3985.

ILO (International Labour Office). Forthcoming. *Non-standard forms of employment*, Report for the Tripartite Meeting of Experts (Geneva).

ILO (International Labour Office); DSS (Department for Statistics and Sociology of the Republic of Moldova). 2004. *Employment in the informal economy in the Republic of Moldova*, Working Paper 41 (Geneva).

ILO (International Labour Office); IILS (International Institute for Labour Studies). 2008. *World of Work Report 2008: Income inequalities in the age of financial globalization* (Geneva).

ILO (International Labour Organization); OECD (Organisation for Economic Co-operation and Development); World Bank. 2014. *G20 labour markets: Outlook, key challenges and policy responses.* Report prepared for the G20 Labour and Employment Ministerial Meeting, Melbourne, Australia, 10–11 Sep.

IMF (International Monetary Fund). 2007. "The globalization of labor", in *World Economic Outlook*, Apr.: *Spillovers and cycles in the world economy* (Washington, DC), pp. 161–92.

IMF (International Monetary Fund). 2013a. *Germany: 2013 Article IV consultation*, IMF Country Report No. 13/255, Aug. (Washington, DC).

IMF (International Monetary Fund). 2013b. *Japan: 2013 Article IV consultation*, IMF Country Report No. 13/253, Aug. (Washington, DC).

IMF (International Monetary Fund). 2013c. World Economic Outlook Database, Oct.

IMF (International Monetary Fund). 2014a. *United States: 2014 Article IV consultation*, IMF Country Report No. 14/221, July (Washington, DC).

IMF (International Monetary Fund). 2014b. *Fiscal policy and income inequality* (Washington, DC).

Immervoll, H. 2009. Minimum-Income Benefits in OECD Countries: Policy Design, Effectiveness and Challenges, IZA DP No. 4627.

Immervoll, H.; Pearson, M. 2009. *A good time for making work pay? Taking stock of in-work benefits and related measures across the OECD*, IZA Policy Paper No. 3.

Jencks, C. 2002. "Does inequality matter?", in *Daedalus*, Vol. 131, No. 1, Winter, pp. 49–65.

Jeong, Y.; Gastwirth, J.L. 2010. *Comments on the draft ILO report "Estimation of global wage trends: Methodological issues"*, mimeo (Washington, DC, HEC Montreal and George Washington University).

Karabarbounis, L.; Neiman, B. 2014. "The global decline of the labor share", in *The Quarterly Journal of Economics*, 129(1), pp. 61–103.

Keifman, S.N.; Maurizio, R. 2012. *Changes in labour market conditions and policies: Their impact on wage inequality during the last decade*, United Nations University World Institute for Development Economics Research (UNU-WIDER), Working Paper 2012/14 (Helsinki).

Kharas, H. 2010. *The emerging middle class in developing countries*, Working Paper 285 (Paris, OECD Development Centre).

Krueger, A. 2012. "The rise and consequences of inequality in the United States", speech at the Center for American Progress, Washington, DC, 12 Jan.

Kumhof, M.; Rancière, R. 2010. *Inequality, leverage and crises*, Working Paper 10/268 (Washington, DC, IMF).

Lavoie, M.; Stockhammer, E. (eds). 2013. *Wage-led growth: An equitable strategy for economic recovery* (Geneva and Basingstoke, ILO and Palgrave Macmillan).

Lazear, E.P.; Rosen, S. 1981. "Rank-order tournaments as optimum labor contracts", in *Journal of Political Economy*, Vol. 89, No. 5, pp. 841–64.

Lee, S.; McCann, D. 2014. "Regulatory indeterminacy and protection in contemporary labour markets: Innovation in research and policy", in D. McCann, S. Lee, P. Belser, C. Fenwick, J. Howe and M. Luebker (eds): *Creative labour regulation: Indeterminacy and protection in an uncertain world* (Geneva and Basingstoke, ILO and Palgrave Macmillan), pp. 3–28.

Leonard, M.; Stanley, T.D.; Doucouliagos, H. 2013. "Does the UK minimum wage reduce employment? A meta-regression analysis", in *British Journal of Industrial Relations*, Vol. 52, No. 3, pp. 499–520.

López-Calva, L.; Lustig, N. (eds). 2010. *Declining inequality in Latin America: A decade of progress?* (New York and Washington, DC, UNDP and Brookings Institution Press).

Low Pay Commission, 2014. *National minimum wage*, Low Pay Commission Report 2013, Cm 8816, Apr. (London, The Stationery Office).

Lucidi, F.; Kleinknecht, A. 2010. "Little innovation, many jobs: An econometric analysis of the Italian labour productivity crisis", in *Cambridge Journal of Economics*, Vol. 34, No. 3, pp. 525–46.

Lukyanova, A. 2011. *Effects of minimum wages on the Russian wage distribution*, Working Paper WP BRP 09/EC/2011 (National Research University Higher School of Economics, Moscow).

Lukyanova, A. Forthcoming. *Analysis of trends in the distribution of wages in the Russian Federation*, Conditions of Work and Employment Series (Geneva, ILO).

Machado, A.; Perez Ribas, R. 2010. "Do changes in the labour market take families out of poverty? Determinants of exiting poverty in Brazilian metropolitan regions", in *Journal of Development Studies*, Vol. 46, No. 9, pp. 1503–22.

Machin, S. 2009. "Education and inequality", in W. Salverda, B. Nolan and T. Smeeding (eds), pp. 406–31.

Marinakis, A. 2014. *Incumplimiento con el salario mínimo en América Latina: El peso de los factores económicos e institucionales* (Geneva, ILO).

Martins, P.S.; Solon, G.; Thomas, J.P. 2012. "Measuring what employers do about entry wages over the business cycle: A new approach", in *American Economic Journal: Macroeconomics*, Vol. 4, No. 4, pp. 36–55.

Mehran, F. 2010. *Estimation of global wage trends: Methodological issues*, mimeo (Geneva, ILO).

Migone, A. 2007. "Hedonistic consumerism: Patterns of consumption in contemporary capitalism", in *Review of Radical Political Economics*, Vol. 39, No. 2, pp. 173–200.

Milanovic, B. 2011. *The haves and the have-nots: A brief and idiosyncratic history of global inequality* (New York, Basic Books).

Mincer, J. 1974. *Schooling, experience and earnings* (New York, National Bureau of Economic Research).

Nataraj, S.; Perez-Arce, F.; Srinivasan, S.; Kumar, K.B. 2012. *What is the impact of labour market regulations in LICs? How does it vary by gender?* RAND, Labour and Population Working Paper No. 957 (Santa Monica, CA, RAND).

Naughton, B. 2007. *The Chinese economy: Transitions and growth* (Cambridge, MA, and London, MIT Press).

Neves, P.C.; Silva, S.T. 2014. "Inequality and growth: Uncovering the main conclusions from the empirics", in *Journal of Development Studies*, Vol. 50, No. 1, pp. 1–21.

OECD (Organisation for Economic Co-operation and Development). 2001. *Measuring productivity: OECD manual* (Paris).

OECD (Organisation for Economic Co-operation and Development). 2008. *Growing unequal? Income distribution and poverty in OECD countries* (Paris).

OECD (Organisation for Economic Co-operation and Development). 2011. *Divided we stand: Why inequality keeps rising* (Paris).

OECD (Organisation for Economic Co-operation and Development). 2012a. *Employment Outlook 2012* (Paris).

OECD (Organisation for Economic Co-operation and Development). 2012b. *Economic Policy Reforms: Going for growth 2012* (Paris).

OECD (Organisation for Economic Co-operation and Development). 2014a. *All on board: Making inclusive growth happen* (Paris).

OECD (Organisation for Economic Co-operation and Development). 2014b. *Employment Outlook 2014* (Paris).

Ostry, J.D.; Berg, A.; Tsangarides, C.G. 2014. *Redistribution, inequality, and growth*, Discussion Note SDN/14/02 (Washington, DC, IMF).

Oyvat, C. 2011. "Globalization, wage shares and income distribution in Turkey", in *Cambridge Journal of Regions, Economy and Society*, Vol. 4, No. 1, pp. 123–38.

Palley, T.I.; Horn, G.A. (eds). 2013. *Restoring shared prosperity: A policy agenda from leading Keynesian economists* (CreateSpace Independent Publishing).

Perotti, R. 1996. "Growth, income distribution, and democracy: What the data say", *Journal of Economic Growth*, Vol. 1, No. 2, pp. 149–87.

Piketty, T. 2013. *Le capital au XXI*[e] *siècle* (Paris, Seuil).

Rajan, R. 2010. *Fault lines: How hidden fractures still threaten the world economy* (Princeton, NJ, Princeton University Press).

Rand, J.; Torm, N. 2012. "The benefits of formalization: Evidence from Vietnamese manufacturing SMEs", in *World Development*, Vol. 40, No. 5, May, pp. 983–98.

Rani, U.; Belser, P.; Oelz, M.; Ranjbar, S. 2013. "Minimum wage coverage and compliance in developing countries", in *International Labour Review*, Vol. 152, No. 3–4, Special Issue, *Informality across the global economy – subsistence, avoidance and violation* (Geneva, ILO).

Rao, S.; Sharpe, A.; Smith, J. 2005. "An analysis of the labour productivity growth slowdown in Canada since 2000", in *International Productivity Monitor*, No. 10, Spring, pp. 3–23.

Ravallion, M. 2010. "The developing world's bulging (but vulnerable) middle class", in *World Development*, Vol. 38, No. 4, pp. 445–54.

Rodrik, D. 1999. "Where did all the growth go? External shocks, social conflict, and growth collapses", in *Journal of Economic Growth*, Vol. 4, No. 4, pp. 385–412.

Rubery, J. 2003. *Pay equity, minimum wage and equality at work*, InFocus Programme on Promoting the Declaration on Fundamental Principles and Rights at Work, Working Paper DECLARATION/WP/19/2003 (Geneva, ILO).

Rubery, J.; Grimshaw, D.; Figueiredo, H. 2005. "How to close the gender pay gap in Europe: Towards the gender mainstreaming of pay policy", in *Industrial Relations Journal*, Vol. 36, No. 3, pp. 184–213.

Salverda, W.; Nolan, B.; Smeeding, T. (eds). 2009a. *The Oxford handbook of economic inequality* (Oxford, Oxford University Press).

Salverda, W.; Nolan, B.; Smeeding, T. 2009b. "Introduction", in W. Salverda, B. Nolan and T. Smeeding (eds), pp. 3–23.

Särndal, C.-E.; Deville, J.-C. 1992. "Calibration estimators in survey sampling?", in *Journal of the American Statistical Association*, Vol. 87, No. 418, pp. 376–82.

Sharpe, A.; Arsenault, J.-F.; Harrison, P. 2008. *The relationship between labour productivity and real wage growth in Canada and OECD countries*, Research Report 2008-8 (Ottawa, Centre for the Study of Living Standards).

Sobeck, K. Forthcoming. *Trends in wages and productivity in developed economies*, Conditions of Work and Employment series (Geneva, ILO).

Solé, C.; Parella, S. 2003. "The labour market and racial discrimination in Spain", in *Journal of Ethnic and Migration Studies*, Vol. 29, No. 1, pp. 121–40.

Solon, G.; Barsky, R.B.; Parker, J.A. 1994. "Measuring the cyclicality of real wages: How important is composition bias?", in *Quarterly Journal of Economics*, Vol. 109, No. 1, Feb., pp. 1–25.

Sommer, M. 2009. *Why are Japanese wages so sluggish?*, Working Paper WP/09/97 (Washington, DC, IMF).

Statistics Canada. 2014. Table 281-0063 – Employment and average weekly earnings including overtime (SEPH), seasonally adjusted, for all employees by industries classified using the North American Industry Classification System (NAICS), annual (persons unless otherwise noted) [29 Oct. 2014].

Sturn, S.; Van Treeck, T. 2013. "The role of income inequality as a cause of the Great Recession and global imbalances", in M. Lavoie and E. Stockhammer (eds), pp. 125–52.

Tansel, A.; Bircan, F. 2010. "Wage inequality and returns to education in Turkey: A quantile regression analysis", Discussion Paper 5417 (Bonn, IZA).

Tansel, A.; Kan, E.O. 2012. "The Formal/Informal Employment Earnings Gap: Evidence from Turkey", Discussion Paper 6556 (Bonn, IZA).

Tillé, Y. 2001. *Théorie des sondages: Echantillonage et estimation en populations finies* (Paris, Dunod).

Tillé, Y. 2010. *Expertise report on the "Estimation of global wage trends: Methodological issues"*, mimeo (Neuchâtel, Institute of Statistics, University of Neuchâtel).

Trentmann, F. 2004. "Beyond consumerism: New historical perspectives on consumption", in *Journal of Contemporary History*, Vol. 39, No. 3, pp. 373–401.

Tronti, L. 2010. "The Italian productivity slow-down: The role of the bargaining model", in *International Journal of Manpower*, Vol. 31, Issue 7, pp. 770–92.

UNdata. 2014. National accounts data. Available at: http://data.un.org/ [8 Aug. 2014].

UNECE (United Nations Economic Commission For Europe). 2011. *Canberra Group handbook on household income statistics,* 2nd edn (Geneva, United Nations). Available at: http://www.unece.org/fileadmin/DAM/stats/groups/cgh/Canbera_Handbook_2011_WEB.pdf [22 Sep. 2014].

USCEA (United States Council of Economic Advisers). 2014. *The economic report of the President together with the annual report of the Council of Economic Advisers, 2014* (Washington, DC, US Government Printing Office).

Van Biesebroeck, J. Forthcoming. *How tight is the link between wages and productivity? A survey of the literature*, Conditions of Work and Employment series (Geneva, ILO).

Verma, V.; Betti, G. 2010. "Data accuracy in EU-SILC", in A.B. Atkinson and E. Marlier (eds): *Income and living conditions in Europe* (Luxembourg, Publications Office of the European Union), pp. 57–77.

Visser, J.; Checchi, D. 2009. "Inequality and the labor market: Unions", in W. Salverda, B. Nolan and T. Smeeding (eds), pp. 230–57.

Wittenberg, M. 2014. *Analysis of employment, real wage, and productivity trends in South Africa since 1994*, Conditions of Work and Employment Series 45 (Geneva, ILO).

Wolf, M. 2014a. *The shifts and the shocks: What we've learned – and have still to learn – from the financial crisis* (London, Penguin).

Wolf, M. 2014b. Reform alone is no solution for the Eurozone, *Financial Times*, 21 Oct.

World Bank. 1999. *Russia: Targeting and the longer-term poor*, Report 19377-RU (Washington, DC).

World Bank. 2006. *World Development Report 2006: Equity and development* (Washington, DC, and Oxford, World Bank and Oxford University Press).

World Bank. 2012. "Overview", in *World Development Report 2012: Gender equality and development* (Washington, DC), pp. 2–40.

Yellen, J.L. 2014. "Labor market dynamics and monetary policy", speech given at the Federal Reserve Bank of Kansas City Economic Symposium, Jackson Hole, Wyoming, 22 Aug. Available at: http://www.federalreserve.gov/newsevents/speech/yellen20140822a.htm [22 Sep. 2014].